The power of products

The power of products

How Finnish companies discovered the secret of global product strategy, and how this discovery transformed the industry

Kari Leppälä

The power of products:
How Finnish companies discovered the secret of global product strategy,
and how this discovery transformed the industry

Kari Leppälä

© 2007

Rights owner: Kari Leppälä

Publisher: Lulu.com

ISBN 978-1-84753-596-2

Preface

The modern world is technical. Everyday life depends essentially on technical products. The modern urban infrastructure relies critically on technology: transportation, communication, housing, clothing, and energy and food supply, communication and information resources depend on availability and functionality of technology. We need and utilize technology to accomplish our everyday tasks. Even our leisure time is increasingly technical. Advancing technology has created sophisticated devices and systems, which require continuous attention of expert professionals for maintenance and renovation.

The global technological life style is the fruit of the industrial revolution. During the early centuries of industrialization, the superiority of the industrial style of value creation was based on production efficiency. At the same time, the quality and functionality of factory made products was in most cases far better than with artisan made products. However, in the 21st century, the industrial landscape has changed. Production capability has become like a commodity, it can be acquired upon need, and it is available for every one. Now competition is, more than ever, based on product performance.

Joseph Schumpeter, one of the great economists of the 20th century, explained the dynamics of technological change. Industrial competition capability is achieved through technological innovations. Companies which cannot create new technologies or adopt them become the victims of "creative destruction". And ultimately, the industrial value process is supplied by consumer markets: consumer acceptance determines, which companies survive.

It appears that the strategy focus of industry is shifting from manufacturing and marketing capability towards product and service based strategies. According to our view, the companies which can create and distribute products with customer and consumer focus will prosper. Except logically, this claim can be supported through a special case. We will describe, how Finnish companies in a few decades discovered the secret of modern product based strategy, and how this discovery changed the entire industry. The Nokia company is famous for its phenomenal success in mobile phone industry, and many readers know, that Nokia originated from Finland. We will describe, how Nokia, together with other successful companies could utilize the local resources, environment and culture, and made a breakthrough into global markets, by offering excellent products. In parallel with this process, and partially as a result, an industrial transformation took place, and created a modern, global and industrial information age economy.

Our viewpoint is deliberately limited. We largely by-pass the strategy textbook approach, where markets are mature, competition is hard, and products are roughly similar. Under such conditions, established business and marketing strategies are relevant. There are also strategies for dominating markets by creating and acquiring control over key infrastructure elements or resources: standards, knowledge, resources, and key products, often referred as business platforms. These complicated issues are not treated in detail. The aim of this book is to describe elements of technology and product based strategies with a customer focus.

Being technically innovative may become a receipt of success. We consider a process, where a company penetrates into global markets by offering new, high-class products. Each of the four industrial cases involves a novelty, which the case company is able to utilize. In the mobile phone case, it is a new, evolving product innovation. But it may as well be, like in the other cases, on a mature business area, and the novelty is a new quality and performance class. And in each case, the effect is created through application of new technology and excellent product engineering. Like many other analysts, we first considered the Nokia case anomalous, but when we started to investigate other industrial cases, a repeating pattern[1] was found. The phenomenon is so striking, that it can be seen as a strategy option. We call this option "the product excellence strategy".

In the first and second parts of the book, there are two related themes, which run in parallel. We explore the world which is dominated by industrial products. Using a light historical touch we describe, how industrial products have shaped our world, and are changing it continuously. We also describe how companies operate in close interaction with the entire society. At the same time, industry is the active contributor to the technological change, and is trying to take a share of the new value

---

[1] Of course, the Finnish cases are not unique. It is easy to point out roughly similar examples: the Macintosh computer, Sony Walkman, the Swiss army knife etc. An especially illuminating and well-known case is the introduction of the Xerox copy machine (a novel product innovation based on new technology), and its defeat by Canon twenty years later (introducing a new product and quality class).

processes that emerge of the use and impacts of technology. The topic of the second part is, how engineers design new products, how they manage the associated information and knowledge, and what kind of tools and methods they use. Actually, at first we tried to keep the society viewpoint and industry and business viewpoints completely separate. However, those views are so closely related, that there is same overlapping.

It is also necessary to analyze changes in technology. Advances in electronics and microprocessor technology have introduced new functionality in products. New products are no longer passive tools and facilitators. They access information resources and communication channels, and interact and communicate with their human masters, adapting to their needs and providing personalized services. Humans have a tendency to anthropomorphize things, and we like to consider the new products smart companions rather than dull machines.

A large portion of the functionality of new products is created through software. As a generic and versatile technology, software engineering has gained considerable importance. Among the challenges in new product design, software is in a curious position. Unlike any other engineering discipline, software is the only one which is an inherently non-visual craft. Engineers are shifting towards utilizing computer aided tools such as CAD, to facilitate and empower their working procedures. Software engineering has been fully computerized practically from the very beginning. Software is technically speaking a collection of lines of artificial, abstract programming language. The result of software design is a mass of program code, which is too often incomprehensible even to the rest of the product design team.

One solution for managing design, and especially software design might be to re-establish and empower the traditional and well-proven visual engineering language for product design. The essence of the idea is that a functional visual product model should be created from the very beginning of the design project by applying two and three-dimensional computer graphics. This model is then utilized as a central communication platform and focus of activity during the subsequent phases of design refinement.

Part III of the book introduces the four industrial cases. It combines the description of political and social situation in the society, with background information of the companies. Each innovation is described, and especially, it is evaluated from the end user perspective. How the product was received, how it is used, and what is the real advantage that the product offers. An important question is, what is the future of the product- and technology-based approach? Can it survive current migration of activities into low-cost countries? What is the role of nationality, local resources, and local culture?

The style of the book is not strictly scientific treatise, and we try to avoid being over-technical. We share the opinion that language with all its inaccuracies and especially its style aspects with rhetoric tones and emotional load is a most important vehicle for sharing information and understanding. We have used in a narrative voice, but also want to follow principles of exact technical and scientific documentation. When we discuss culture, and social and psychological issues, it is anyway difficult to be accurate in the sense common in sciences.

By permission of the publisher, this book contains material of a former book: Kari Leppälä, Mikko Kerttula and Tuomo Tuikka: "Virtual design of smart products", Edita 2003. It is not a re-print, but the book is thoroughly re-organized. Detailed presentation of virtual design techniques and tools has been removed, the industrial cases section is extended and new cases introduced. The entire book is revised or re-written.

Oulu, June 2007

Kari Leppälä

Contents

Part I
World of innovations

Introduction to product ecology

Products are essential companions and facilitators of everyday life. New products have to fit commercial, technological, social and psychological aspects. Product design requires application of versatile technical skills. But products are not simply a form of output for industrial activity. Participating in product teams is not just unstructured team work, guided by intuition and group dynamics. The members of a product team take certain roles, and engineering practices take a very specific form. To understand and explain, why engineers and designers work how they do, it is illustrative to begin our exploration by considering how technology and engineering practices have emerged in the course of history.

Among our information sources we want to highlight E. Ferguson's book "Engineering and the Mind's Eye" [8], which combines the evolution of engineering practices with the viewpoint of visual language.

Technical society emerges in Europe

The human world has always been technology-augmented. We can even claim that human evolution has been shaped by technology. For example, the structure of human hands and the erect body position are ideal for using tools, and the lack of protective body hair indicates continued use of clothing and shelter. However, the forms of creating and distributing technology have changed. For our ancestors, technology was necessary for survival, and for making life easier - or at least tolerable. Especially in cold climates, housing, heating, food processing technology and food preservation ensured minimum living conditions. Living was supported by outdoor technologies: fishing, hunting and agriculture. Communication and transportation technologies were developed to share local resources with distant members of the species. Sharing and exchange of resources and products has taken place peacefully in the context trade - and sometimes less peacefully.

The eve of professional engineering in the modern sense started to gain momentum in Renaissance Italy starting from the 15th century [2]. The era introduced a radical change in the working conventions of product creation. Renaissance masters developed a rich visual presentation style to describe technology and its application. At the time and long afterwards, artisans were trained into their profession through personal learning in the workshops of old masters. The process was almost entirely guided by oral tradition, learning in work tasks and examining existing work items. However, while the word "engineer" was finding use to denote persons, devoted for inventing and applying of special artifacts, engineering came into existence as a visual art. Practically all the aspects of engineering diagrams were present in the beautifully drafted engineering drawings by Leonardo da Vinci: perspective and projections, enlarged illustrations of details and declarative notes. The Renaissance masters also described technology in action: drawings of pumps, elevators, water mills and sawmills were presented in operation, with their surroundings and operators. Notebooks of engineers, as well as special picture books and encyclopedias of technical components were copied, printed and distributed. Italian engineering masters traveled throughout Europe making this new craft and art known all over the continent.

Of course, engineering became a visual art for pragmatic reasons. It was necessary to present and promote the plans of machines and military systems to the patrons, the powerful Renaissance noblemen. The engineer was too busy in acquiring funding and monitoring the projects, and needed other professionals - fine smiths and carpenters - to build the actual devices. Thus, drawings were also needed to provide instructions for the prototype workshop. Together with the engineers, another modern profession was emerging: technicians.

Today, we know that many of Leonardo's creations, for example, the helicopter and the automobile did not function correctly in practice. A final element of modern engineering was missing. Except trial and error, there were few methods or mental aids for justifying engineers' inventions. For example, Leonardo was not able to calculate the energy needed to operate his machines. Actually, he did not even have the concept of

---

[2] We find the discussion of the European technology history illustrative for understanding the origin and fundamentals of industrial technology, because it is well documented and more or less familiar. However, we remind, that pre-industrial technology has been developed by various societies since the ancient times. The foundation of science was set by Indians, Babylonians, Egyptians, Greeks and Arabs, and before the breakthrough of industrial revolution, technology was flowing to Europe for centuries, especially from China.

energy; not until the era of Galileo, Leibniz, Descartes, Newton and many others, who combined mathematics with engineering.

Instead of analysis, renaissance engineers often applied "professional judgment" to justify their decisions. When Michelangelo designed the imposing St. Peter's main cupola in 1547, he relied on his knowledge of similar constructions. In addition, several detailed wooden and clay models were made to study the design and to provide guidance for constructors. The cupola was finished after Michelangelo's death in altered form, and was soon showing signs of damage because of insufficient construction strength. Two hundred years later a survey was made of the condition of the cupola, and mathematical analysis was used to calculate the stress. The analysis was objected "because Michelangelo knew nothing of mathematics and was still able to create the dome." Despite hard criticism, five supporting rings made of iron were assembled to save the cupola.

Centuries later, James Watt still had problems with understanding the steam engine. He could not calculate the efficiency of the machine, because the theory of thermodynamics emerged later - actually it was inspired by the work of steam engine pioneers. However, Watt was on the right track: he could intuitively understand and apply some principles of thermodynamics in their early form, and was able to radically improve the efficiency of the steam engine. He accomplished it not by exact analysis, but through experimentation, which was guided by pre-scientific hypotheses. Modern engineers support their analysis with professional judgment, and sometimes also replace the analysis with judgment. Obviously, this happens because exact analysis is still a challenging, difficult and error-prone task. Especially software engineers rarely rely on analysis, although methods such as state simulation and formal proof are available.

Since the introduction of mathematical analysis, all the elements of modern engineering were formed, and the intellectual base for the industrial revolution was ready [3]. Among the first landmarks of the new industrial technology was Thomas Newcomen's atmospheric steam engine water pump. Although hopelessly inefficient, this giant machine was no longer a curiosity, but a serious and profitable production device. The engine was still created by crafts methods, and trial and error. The few remaining original drawings of the engine were made in Renaissance style and were drafted afterwards. James Watt opened a new era with his systematic engineering practices, and accurate and detailed drawings. The

[3] In parallel with emerging technology, another modern practice was emerging: sciences. Perhaps the successful application of analysis in practical technical problems encouraged extending the methods of analysis towards more abstract purposes: to explain the phenomena of nature. Since the 17th century, technology and sciences created a complex, mutual and interactive relationship.

new engineering drawing practice set foundations of modern visual engineering, and created the superior, high-quality and highly efficient steam engine.

The modern steam engine was a definitive and irreversible turn of history. Industrial scale production with machines and energy, instead of masses of artisans, was a strong business opportunity, which had both fascinating and disturbing consequences. The Renaissance artist-engineer was replaced by the organizer-industrializer engineer. The great engineers of the industrialization period, e.g. Henry Ford, Thomas Edison, Werner von Siemens and Alfred Nobel established and managed their industrial emporiums.

Nothing remains unchanged except change itself. Today, the focus of industry has again shifted from production to products. The renaissance legacy artist-inventor-engineers are again called to the front line. The inventor-engineer first turned into an industrialist. But today, as product design becomes more important, artist-engineers may be needed once again.

Product teams enter the scene

One characteristic feature of the modern world is the specialization and segregation of professions. Citizens are subdivided between two roles. They are either the consumers or producers of everyday artifacts. Among producers, there is more segregation. To create a new product, a product team of specialized professionals is set up.

The composition of a product team reflects both the environment of the product, and the technology, which makes up and empowers the product. We talk of engineers as persons who plan and arrange product creation processes, and of designers as persons who participate in the core of product creation. We have also distinguished between design and production processes, and usually it is also necessary to include a special prototyping function between design and production phases. There are also different kinds of designers. A mechanical designer creates structures to create the physical product frame and mechanical functions. An electronics designer designs the electronic control structure of the product, and because current products often contain microprocessors, we also need software developers. An industrial designer gives the product its final, attractive form and appearance. It is noteworthy that of the above professionals all except the industrial designer have trained as engineers.

If we consider the evolution of product design practices, we notice two historically new members in the design team: the software designer and the industrial designer. Their roles are opposite in a peculiar way. The software designer tends to be at least professionally introverted. He tends to think of the product entirely in terms of software, and is often accused of ignoring the end user. His work is in some sense near alchemy: because of the non-visual nature of software, other team members have difficulty understanding what he is doing, and how his share of the work is progressing.

The industrial designer in turn seems to professionally be an extrovert. It appears to be his task to fit and adjust the product to the external world. He is the person who already in the early phases of design negotiates with the user, and with the marketing department and management. On the other hand, he is usually not technically trained, and many criticize his work for this reason. As his profession lacks the secrets of a technical profession, he may choose to highlight the mystery of artistic creativity.

The digital age

Whether we recognize it or not, technology has taken become an indispensable element of everyday life. However, during the recent decades, an important change has taken place. No longer is it the everyman, supported by skilful artisans and hand workers, who acquires and maintains the necessary everyday devices and appliances. The creation of technical artifacts and systems has turned into a specialized profession of the engineers. At the same time, the provision of new products has become a worldwide commercial business activity. Product companies are definitely the economical landmarks of our time.

Industrialization created a completely new technological infrastructure. First, the technological infrastructure was created through large-scale production of materials, energy and production machines. A parallel task was the creation of communication infrastructure for society, in the form of efficient steam and combustion engine powered ships, trains, automobiles and electrical communication networks. Consumer goods were also produced: clothing, packaged foods, and different tools and appliances. Consumers were buying industrial products, to use them as tools and for everyday commodities.

What is the present situation? Has new information technology introduced change in global markets? A general trend is cost-efficiency. Energy and materials are produced more economically and using natural resources more efficiently. A new energy infrastructure is not yet available, but considering the diminishing fuel resources and ecological concerns, the energy sector is waiting to be re-designed. The transportation infrastructure is still growing: the ever increasing automobile density and continuously growing road networks challenge the structure of societies and global ecology. Again, information technology is called to mitigate the economical and ecological consequences of technological progress. At the core of the change, the consumer of today - the everyman - is more dependent on technology than ever. There is a shift from a tool user towards buying and using ready-made products in every sector of life.

In the information sector, we are witnessing the emergence of a new information infrastructure, where the leading principle is digitalization. During the last 25 years, we have seen how traditional "analogue" information systems have been replaced with digital counterparts. For example, vinyl records have effectively been replaced by the CD and DVD and solid state memories. And the content will be enclosed by MP3, MPEG and other packaging technologies, which work on a diversity of platforms and distribution media. Telephone networks in industrialized countries have become digital (which admittedly is invisible to consumers), and radio telephones, and now also conventional telephones are being replaced with cellular mobile phone systems. Now that the basic infrastructure is practically digital, a new development phase is emerging. A generic feature of a digital application is media independence. A telephone call or a multimedia message may take any logical form (coding and protocol) and any physical path (cellular radio, wideband link, cable network or satellite). The application can also use any terminal device: we can make a phone call using a computer, and send a text or multimedia message with a mobile phone. This migration of digital applications is only restricted by artificial limitations, typically set by available commercial resources and services - or regulation or censorship actions.

Like every past generation, we are facing a restless and insecure future. Our generation witnesses, how the technological production system and modern life style are progressing on a global scale. This means new users and markets for industrial consumer products. It is also a global social and ecological issue. It is even possible, that the basic energy and raw materials industry of the future will compete for sparse intellectual and capital resources with the consumer product industry. The consumer products industry is confronting a fundamental and currently unanswered question: what will be the physical and logical form of new digital consumer applications?

Design - the key process of modern industry

Design as a whole is a goal oriented process, which aims to produce a new technical artifact - a product to be manufactured with industrial methods and on an industrial scale. The ultimate purpose of the product is to be used by a customer to fulfill more or less serious needs. As we will discuss, a design may be an entirely new, radical design, or a modification of some earlier, already existing product. Actually, nearly all new designs are of the latter type. Regardless of the novelty of the design, the content of designing is more or less the same, involving different human activities and capabilities.

One way of illustrating the situation of designing is given in Figure 1. First of all, we have two complementary ways of considering designing. We may view it as a systematic, rational process, which can be explicitly described, subdivided into life cycle phases, and further into parallel and sequential tasks. The other viewpoint is that of cognition science. Here we see designing as an activity, which rearranges and manipulates information. The designer is seen as a system which is capable of interpreting and manipulating information.

The systematic design process has different activities. On top of other activities, we may apply a meta-activity called process management, which shapes the articulation of other activity types. Functional design means the decomposition and extension of the design task into product functions. Functions describe in a relatively abstract manner the service and utility the product is supposed to provide. Form design denotes a design phase, which transforms the design functions and other external requirements into realization components. Form is understood to denote both the external shape of the product, and the totality and interconnections of its technical components. Finally, between the systematic and cognitive portions, there is the design rationale, which aims to explain, why the product is constructed a certain way.

On the psychological and cognitive side we try to understand and conceptualize those human capabilities that make designing possible. Especially, we are interested to find ways to support the design process: through proper organization of work, appropriate information resources, and computerized support techniques.

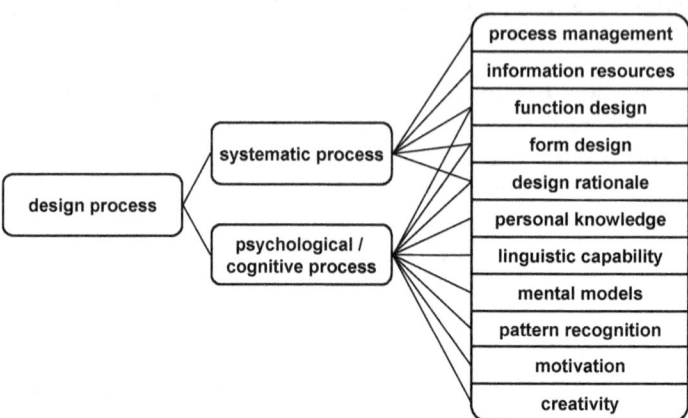

Figure 1. Design related categories.

From the individual perspective, we aim for better understanding and more effective performance of the design task, and from a social perspective we want to improve the transfer of ideas and promote the creation of shared understanding in the design team. Since the early ages of computer technology, research on computer supported collaborative work (CSCW) has been working on these issues. Advances in this research area have to be considered against the application background. In order to support reasoning, we should understand how design rationales are expressed, and to emphasize knowledge management we should understand the nature of technical knowledge.

Innovations and infrastructures

We will take a closer look at the technological change, which is a continuing and cumulative progress on new technologies and new innovations. We emphasize the modern concepts and terminology of innovations and inventions, as they were proposed already around 1920 by Josepf Schumpeter [25]. We also discuss the concept of "infrastructure." Technical products are not independent and usually require a sophisticated support and service network. We believe that infrastructure is one key concept for understanding the dynamics of product innovations.

It has been claimed, that when inhabitants living on a distant and isolated island first see a modern ship, they are completely incapable of describing it, or even drawing a picture. In light of current knowledge, it seems understandable. Human thinking is based on metaphors: when we describe something new, we need to refer to existing models and analogies. As has been concretely demonstrated by futurological studies and forecasts made in the 1960s, even the best specialists are surprisingly helpless when trying to predict the future development of technology. Nevertheless, we will attempt to characterize future technologies and products.

A number of studies have been made about metaphoric thinking and mental models [10, 13]. Science fiction literature, especially the "cyberpunk" genre and William Gibson have inspired information product designers [28]. We also mention visionary product proposals from the past: the "memex" multimedia concept by Vannevar Bush [4] in 1945, and Ted Nelson's "Xanadu" [18], which summarizes original ideas and the term "hypertext" he proposed in 1965. We also refer to the ideas of recent visionaries such as Mark Weiser [34] and Nicholas Negroponte [17]. We use the term "smart product" in a specific meaning: a next generation personal information and media product.

Technical infrastructure as innovation accelerator

We have discussed, how an innovation cannot progress, unless it takes a form and behavior, which are culturally accepted and adopted. This is usually a slow process, and the development of technology has been compared to biological evolution. It takes place in the form of slight modifications and gradual improvements. Only now and then a novel innovation is born, which is capable of utilizing the present product environment, and this way it may also find a faster track.

We will characterize the environment in which the product lives as infrastructure. The cultural and epistemic infrastructure consists of public discussion and common beliefs. New technology requires new kind of professionals, and after a pioneering phase, professional schools and universities begin to offer educational services. The technical infrastructure contains technical elements, which are not part of the product, but are necessary for their utilization. Some products can be used without a technical infrastructure, or the infrastructure has commercial services such as the availability of spare parts, supplies and materials. A hammer presupposes nails, and a portable radio needs batteries and a broadcasting network.

All products require a social and technical infrastructure. However, some products are dependent on a special technical infrastructure. Such an infrastructure will emerge, once the innovation is considered so important that the investments are found necessary. To be more precise, such technical infrastructures are regionally distributed networks, which disseminate energy, information or matter. Transportation routes are an example of the last type. A supplies and services infrastructure usually develops through commercial activity and minor investments, which are made by product users. However, large regional networks are entirely different, and require large investments.

Who is responsible for building the infrastructure in a typical situation, where products and services are still marginal and cannot provide added value for investments? How to allocate the possible economical advantage of operating the network, if the network is not built by operators? How to create justification for a network for a new service, which is mostly unknown to the majority of consumers? A technical network needs a common technical standard so that products can use it. How to agree on the standard, if there are commercial and national interests for which one standard may be more advantageous than for others? No one can answer these controversial questions. Obviously, there is no correct answer, and a feasible answer depends on the situation. We will illustrate possible solutions through familiar examples.

Starting with degraded performance

When radio broadcasting was initiated it was in limited professional use, mainly by the army, and there were no commercial products, or even any paragons. The radio was an entirely novel invention, and the concept was not familiar to consumers. Because radio was important from a military perspective and for national safety, in most countries, radio broadcasting was strictly controlled by national governments [4]. It was natural that governments either granted licenses for broadcasting, or established broadcasting companies. The essential principle was, that broadcasting was started using long waves, where the range was long. Only a few transmitter stations were needed per country. This was a low investment policy. Later, when radio became popular, broadcasting was moved to medium wave, and then to VHF wavelengths, which due the short range of transmission allowed more efficient use of radio frequencies. The current radio broadcasting network has much more capacity than the initial long wave radio. Because there was an early international agreement on frequency allocations, radio set manufacturers could equip their receivers with new radio bands even before they were used nationally.

It is reasonable to assume, that when public radio broadcasting was started on long waves, the possibility of network upgrading was not fully realized. It came as a by-product: a gift of nature and technology. However, it worked well in practice. Of course there were other happy incidents. Radio technology was not very sophisticated. It was accessible for enthusiasts, and radio amateurs helped to propagate the innovation by disseminating knowledge and building radio sets at a time when commercial supply was insufficient. Radio became a successful global innovation, and found its way also to less developed countries.

Starting with limited coverage

Railways need a technical standard (rail gauge) and a new type of infrastructure (iron rails). Railways were initially constructed for local needs. Industrial companies built railway connections to transfer raw materials and products between production units. Railways were also built for communities, to connect nearby population centers. Especially in Great

---

[4] Radio was first considered for military and business use. When radio amateurs initiated public radio broadcasting more than 20 years after the initial inventions, radio became rapidly a popular consumer innovation. Mobile phone has a similar history. It was intended for professional and business users, until Nokia launched several low-price models for the consumer sector. The consequences surprised all.

Britain there were several local railway systems, but no general standard for rail gauge. Obviously, railway owners suffered losses because different railway networks could not be connected. (In some less industrialized countries, such as Finland, the government was the main railway builder [5], and national railway gauge emerged). Limited coverage was not a problem with railways. It was a supplementary innovation, and passengers could combine it with other transportation methods. Because of increasing international cargo traffic, rail gauge standardization became necessary in Europe.

The limited coverage strategy worked well, because there was no real need to standardize locomotives and railway cars. Machine workshops had no difficulty producing small quantities of locomotives and cars for different rail gauges. The infrastructure builder was also the main user. The success of railways was due the utility of railways in general, and not because of benefits of some specific train or car types.

When an infrastructure-dependent product is targeted for consumers, it is economical to start the service in large cities. This is because the infrastructure is a regional network, and in densely populated areas the infrastructure cost per user is lower. Once the infrastructure is in operation, it supports product sales and makes the product familiar. The disadvantage is that limited coverage makes the product less attractive. Even the consumers who live in the covered area are concerned that the infrastructure may be discontinued.

On consumer markets, the experience of limited coverage networks is contradictory. Although successful national networks were first launched in large cities, the operators expressed a firm commitment to provide services throughout the nation. Operators also considered regional coverage so important, that they made roaming agreements with operators in different countries. Roaming agreements guaranteed continuation of service despite national boundaries, and in Europe, network operators advertise roaming agreements as valuable features for consumers.

Using an existing network

Sometimes a new innovation is compatible with traditional ones. Automobiles require a network of good roads. However, they can also use existing streets and roads. Of course, roads were designed for horses and carriages, and self-powered cars could not provide their full performance

---

[5] In 1857 Finland was an autonomic part of Russia, and inherited the railway gauge from the mother country. Finland was also an agricultural, sparsely populated country. In this case the motivation of the technology investment was political: to strengthen the connection between the countries.

on such surfaces. Actually, there where competing car configurations: with electrical motors, combustion engines and even with steam engines. Only when the quality of roads improved and longer journeys became practical, the versatile combustion engine became the industrial standard.

When automobiles were successfully introduced on horse-and-carriage roads, a new market started to emerge. New and better roads were constructed at an increasing pace. Customers who bought automobiles did not pay for roads. Transportation was considered a vital community resource, and the new infrastructure was built mostly with public funds.

The first large telecommunication networks were built for the telephone. Other important telecommunication innovations include the facsimile and telegraph or telex. As inventions they are older than the telephone. However, they remained in restricted use: governments operated telegraph networks mainly between large cities and different countries, and some large newspaper companies had built proprietary facsimile connections or experimented with radio links for transmitting newspaper photographs.

There was a known technical invention, which would have allowed the use of existing telephone networks for facsimile and telegraph applications. This invention was called modulation, and it was originally invented for radio use. Unfortunately, the leading telephone companies resisted the use of telephone networks for facsimile and telegraph. They categorically prohibited connecting third party modulation devices to telephone lines, even though international organizations started publishing modulation standards. The breakthrough in fax terminal business came fifty years after the introduction of modulation- and one hundred and twenty years after the original invention. Not so much because of technology, but because of change of policy, as the telephone companies had to give up resistance. This was too late for the telegraph and telex, as another infrastructure was already replacing them: the Internet.

Infrastructure evolved on its own

The history of the Internet is peculiar and difficult to characterize. It is a vast and complicated system, which was originally created for research purposes without a notion of products or commercial applications. In the early days, the network was intended only for proprietary messages within the military and scientific community. The Internet had no paragon, and the development of its early versions took an unexpected course.

An important origin of the Internet was a defense project in the United States in the 1960s, the Arpanet. The purpose of the project was to develop technology for interconnecting digital computers and their users. The strong idea behind the initiative was a distributed network without a central hub. Information was to be transmitted as a collection of packets, which contained the address of the recipient. This was accomplished through protocol programs, which implemented the rules of handling the packets. In the course of the project, its military character faded out, and packet protocol research spread within the computer science community. Universities and research centers also implemented research results in the form of experimental networks, where researchers and university students could exchange messages. The networks were supported by national science funding authorities, and were established in the United States, Europe, and other parts of the world. Interoperability technologies were also developed, to allow interconnecting different networks, and major computer companies developed industrial network concepts. The actual technical standards, the Internet protocols, were refined, and simple user applications were implemented: electronic mail, discussion groups and file transfer protocols. These applications allowed researchers to exchange messages and data files, and the universities could publish data directories on the network.

The internet was expanding, but it was largely unknown outside the research community. Researchers could use computers and terminals owned by universities, but consumers did not have computers. Another innovation, the personal computer appeared in the 1980s as the next element in the infrastructure. However, consumers and industrial companies could not access the Internet, because the national research funding agencies that supported the backbone networks did not allow commercial provision of network services. This ban was removed in 1991.

The next decisive event came from the European nuclear research center CERN, where a central motivation was to manage the huge mass of technical documents for a certain very large and complicated research facility. This invention was actually the application of several existing concepts. One of the visible elements developed for it was a program for electronic document display, the browser. The electronic document access system, combined with the Internet, created an explosive mixture: the World Wide Web (WWW). In only a few years, the entire academic community had adopted the innovation and soon the industry and consumers also wanted it. It is a historical irony, that the system is not very useful as a technical documentation system. Considering the original objective, the research team at CERN did not succeed very well!

We have described the infrastructure, which is commonly referred as the Internet, but where are the products? There is no easy answer because most products seem to be more possibilities than products. The Internet is an important innovation, but the infrastructure still seems to be more dominant than individual products. As we described, the infrastructure was created, originally with public funding and through cooperation between universities, national governments and telecommunication operators. The Internet has no definitive owner, but is managed and developed by international organizations and task forces, which have been established only for the purpose.

The Internet makes many application products possible. The central products are Web browsers, but fierce competition and free academic software have forced browser manufacturers to distribute their products for free. The truly significant product is a service: the provision of Internet services for consumers and the industry. It is offered by major telecommunication operators, but also by independent service companies. There is an endless number of other, Internet-based products: electronic mail programs, home page generators, Web hotels, electronic commerce platforms, information services, language translation services, education services, application software providers, entertainment providers and data security products.

With regard to our classification, commercial Internet products are an example of our first infrastructure policy case, where an existing infrastructure - a science community network - was used only to get started, and would later be replaced with a proper and more suitable system. The problem is that there are so many potential applications. How to define a satisfactory new standard? An additional complication is that there are also other emerging networks such as wide area radio networks, cellular radio networks, and cable and digital television networks.

It appears, that with the Internet, the infrastructure is abstract: the logical protocol set, and not the physical network. It has the capability to migrate to different physical platforms. Telephone network was originally created to serve a specific product: the telephone. However, as consumers wanted access to internet, telephone companies started to provide internet access through existing telephone wires. Many consumers have already given up the wire telephone, and use the telephone lines only for internet.

Building infrastructure for a pilot product

If a product is attractive enough, it can serve as motivation for building an infrastructure for it. A historical example is the distribution of electric power. Electric power is incredibly important for the industrial world. It has changed the appearance and economy of factories. Versatile electric motors can be used wherever power is needed, instead of clumsy and dangerous mechanical shaft-and-belt power transmission systems. Bright and correctly directed lights make human work safe, and efficient, and a number of warming, heating and automatic control functions are possible. The impact of electricity in homes is as significant.

The advantages of electrical power are obvious to us now, but one hundred years ago the situation was quite different. There was neither recognized need nor a political program to build large power distribution networks. However, society and the industry had a specific and common problem: lighting. Contemporary light sources - oil lamps, and especially in urban areas, gas lamps - were inefficient and hazardous, and they required constant maintenance.

The invention of electric light, and especially the ubiquitous incandescent lamp changed everything. The industry was the first to build local electric systems for lighting purposes. This was natural, as many factories wanted to operate 24 hours a day, and light was needed both indoors and outdoors. The advantages of electrical street lights in cities were recognized. The first solution was to establish a power station and to build a local electric wiring network. Soon consumers also wanted connections to the network. As the demand of power increased, it was to be transmitted from larger and remote power plants, and the building of nationwide networks was initiated. Already in the 1920s, practically all electrical home appliances were in use in industrialized parts of the world. The electrical power infrastructure was created for a pilot product, the electric lamp, and it opened markets for a large family of electrical products.

The telecommunication infrastructure has a similar early history, but development took a different route. Networks for the telephone also started from the industry. The historical involvement of governments in telecommunications was due to national security, and nation wide networks were built by connecting urban areas and strategic military facilities. Consumers adopted the telephone slowly. The networks were operated mostly by national telecommunication monopolies. The same companies also controlled the telephone machine business. Although networks were first automated and then the trunk networks digitalized, new innovations did not emerge on the consumer side. The telephone machine and service remained technically unchanged for about seventy years.

Despite the existence of a global telephone infrastructure, there were no significant business opportunities outside the monopoly of telephone companies. Not until national policies were changed, and telefax and Internet terminals could take advantage of the existing network.

A big-bang start

From a technical viewpoint, the most optimal policy would be to build a full-coverage infrastructure before launching products for it. In such a situation, the infrastructure could provide efficient services from the beginning. It would also boost market ramp-up because the infrastructure building schedule does not slow down the development of markets. In addition, the infrastructure building project would make the innovation known among consumers. However, what is theoretically optimal, may not be so in economical terms. The big-bang approach has several big "ifs."

Infrastructure investments are usually heavy, and investors have probably based the economy of the investment on certain development of business volume. There are many reasons why the business might not develop as predicted. There is the general risk of economical depression, which may delay and limit sales. There is a risk that consumers are not interested in the products. There is a risk of taking a wrong design approach in the infrastructure specification - especially if the infrastructure has novel technical features. There may also be changes in the environment: for example other innovations or political and legislative regulation make the use of the infrastructure less efficient. A reasonable assumption today is that the infrastructure is not built on public funding. Rather, there will be a sufficiently well-supported infrastructure standard, which is preferably also supported by international standardization bodies. The actual construction of the technical infrastructure then rests on a commercial basis. While the risk of failure of an individual investor is smaller in this case, the failure risk of the entire innovation is not reduced at all. Considering risk and success of large infrastructures one could also compare the Global Positioning System (GPS) and the global satellite network Iridium. In this case public investment on GPS, which was motivated by military use of the network, has created a viable and important service. The privately owned Iridium has remained marginal, due low demand of services, and competing projects have been cancelled. The development of European counterpart for GPS, the Galileo project, is initiated, partially due political reasons. The European industry hesitates to support it, and probably more public funding needs to be allocated.

Examples of successful big-bang starts include the Scandinavian mobile telephone network, NMT, and its digital successor, GSM, which is now widely adopted throughout the world. These examples are often referred to and discussed as school examples of the wisdom and rationality of decision makers. However, it is also common wisdom that one cannot learn from successful cases, only unsuccessful ones. A serious initiative regarding high definition television, HDTV, was made at about the same time as the above-mentioned mobile phone networks were initiated, and so far it has been delayed. Consolidation of the HDTV standard has been slow, and during the process, the motivation of national policy makers faded. Presently, a HDTV television standard is emerging as a result of competition within electronics and entertainment industries.

Infrastructure, policy and strategy

The question of infrastructures boils down to two difficult issues: standardization and investment cost. A standard is never a neutral issue. If we take any technical standard, there are always companies and nations who are in a more favorable position than others. Standardization becomes a political and international debate. Standards often contain compromises between technical trade-offs. Efficiency, openness and data security may be on a collision course.

Standards may be created beforehand, to define a uniform commercial platform. When infrastructures emerge through commercial competition, standards are also made afterwards, to create order in chaos. A recent large-scale example of standardizing afterwards was the unification of the voltage on electrical consumer lines within the European Union. Before that, companies had reacted on multiple voltage standards by designing products that operated on different voltages, with additional costs and reduced efficiency, which was of course paid by consumers.

Regarding investment costs, finding the proper policy is extremely difficult. Any policy which allows gradual start-up with low initial investments would be favorable from the consumers' point of view. However, this may lead to the development of incompatible and fragmented infrastructures. Rigid standardization encourages heavy, big-bang type investment policy, which has considerable risks. While companies have learned to listen to consumers in product development, there seems to be little hope that it would take place in infrastructure definition.

Smart products - information access and beyond

We will now discuss totally new type of products, which can for simplicity be called "smart products." These products access information resources through versatile networks, and provide valuable services and utility functions. We are certain that these new products will have considerable significance for the development of our society. They provide society members, be they "consumers" or "producers" with previously unforeseen possibilities for intellectual and emotional activity, exploration, personal and organizational development, and welfare. In this chapter, we try to describe the kind of products we have in mind.

We begin with current and near future products, which we refer to as "media products" because they are used to access and communicate information on different media. We also foresee more advanced, activity oriented products, in which information content is more a mediator, and the products provide entirely new services and utility functions. We call these products simply "smart".

Rethinking the industrial product

How to define a product? Some common features can be distinguished. A product is something desirable and useful. It is an object for trade: something that can be sold and bought, and more importantly, something that is deliberately acquired for this purpose. There are some basic product types: agriculture and food products, and manufactured products such as clothes, appliances and tools. The evolution of culture and economies has also been the evolution of products and production methods. An important milestone was the emergence of industrial production, that is, making products in factories. The tools and machines of the production process are no longer powered by human or animal force, but by an external power source. In modern production, also the control of machines is performed by computers. A human operator cannot compete with computers on speed, accuracy and faultless memory.

Although industrial products are artificial things, there is another, more abstract object of trade: services. Especially in the late industrial period, service has also been treated as a product. Why is this? The answer lies in two practices, which can be applied to both physical artificial objects and utility work called service. The practices are measurement and standardization. An essential property of product-based trade is the ability to specify the product: to make it manageable for the provider and identifiable to the consumer. A product descriptor is the specification, which is essentially a list of qualitative features that describe the utility and function of the product, and quantitative numbers for those features which can be quantified.

A product has to have quantitative features, so that the customer may compare products, and to provide a rational basis for pricing. There are also other conditions for commercial trade. A product has to be identifiable. Products must fall into distinguishable classes, product archetypes. Classification may be based on natural qualities as in food and agricultural products. For example, oil and wine are natural qualities, which serve to identify liquid-like agricultural products. This is more problematic with artificial products. Their classification can be based on a natural feature of utility or usage, but it is not necessarily strict. Tools such as the hammer or knife are identifiable through their different functions, striking and cutting. However, there are intermediate product types, such as the axe. We can claim that, for example, the cutting function is not "natural," but has been made familiar through the use of knives.

Let us take another example. The mobile phone provides a basic utility function: voice communication between two individuals, regardless of their mutual locations. From the history of the telephone, we know that originally, this utility did not serve an inherent human need. Quite the opposite, when the telephone was introduced, it was considered a technical toy: amusing, but not necessary for everyday life. Industrial companies and the military were the first to find uses for the technology, and began building telephone networks. For consumers, it took decades to adopt the idea before really wanting to order telephones to their homes.

The novel development, the mobile phone, is called "mobile" only to clarify a reference to a common metaphor, the "telephone." We call the new device a "cellular," "mobile," "wireless" or "radio" phone only to make the reference more precise. These references are irrelevant from the consumers' viewpoint. Strangely enough, we find that the mobile phone is more fundamental and much closer to the utility of location-independent conversation, than its historical ancestor. This utility is not abstract, but a cultural product, created by the continuous presence of the technical opportunity. The characteristic form and utility function of a product is very much a cultural convention.

Product characterization can be seen as an application of standardization. This is important because trade objects have to be identifiable. There is also another aspect of standardization. An artisan can make products which are of a common type, but the details can vary and be tailored according to customer wishes. In closer consideration, each product is an individual and unique object. The situation changes dramatically, when products are factory made, with automated machines. Now, the product details must also be standardized exactly. Current industrial manufacturing practices possess a built-in trade-off between production capacity and manufacturing cost per unit. Because production capacity is expensive, mass products have to be highly standardized.

The industrial production style has revolutionized markets, by providing customers with both a price and quality advantage. Complicated high technology products such as televisions, video recorders and DVD players can be offered to consumers at affordable prices. At the same time, large scale manufacturing makes it possible to put a lot of effort into product design and manufacturing process design, so that product quality is excellent, and all products are identical. Artisan producers do not have much room in the high-tech era. They do none the less exist, operating in limited fields such as producing individual forms for products or creating user specific special functions. They use the basic industrial product as a platform, or include standard high technology components in their designs.

Innovating is in a paradoxical situation. Utility features, which are the reason for buying a product, are not absolute. They are cultural formations, which have been created by the influence and presence of other products. New and radical inventions have few ancestors, so their utility has not been created or discovered. The form of these inventions is not necessarily natural or fixed. It may change, and usually it will change, if the invention becomes a viable product. Creating new form and utility for a product is the same as creating a standardized specification, but how can this be accomplished, as the standard must be acceptable to both consumers and the technical infrastructure. The product sample must somehow be introduced in public. Pioneering companies bravely introduce pilot products, hoping to set a new product standard and become market leaders. However, success may very well take years or even decades.

Complexity

There is a continuous and historically verifiable tendency that products - and technology - become increasingly complicated. This is evident in many ways: the number of components and features in a product tends to increase, and the accuracy of production increases, and product details become finer and finer. In many business areas in which competition is heavy, companies attempt to improve product performance and functionality through applying electronics and fine feature machine technology. At least in transportation technology and the home appliance industry, product complexity seems to be in growth. One explanation is the enormous development of microelectronic circuit production technology, which has been made possible by the increasing demand of electronics products such as personal computers. The progress has been impressive because semiconductor technology is still immature, and an intrinsic technology development is in progress. If single transistors are counted, a typical electronics product contains tens of millions of parts. A specific feature of microelectronic components is that the production process is very efficient: millions of components are integrated on chips in one processing batch. The real effort is in design. However, to remove some mysticism from microelectronics technology, it is illuminating to know that the enormous part counts are reached through copying techniques: once a small number of basic functional units have been designed and verified, they can be replicated thousands or millions of times, with the aid of computer-based tools.

A similar phenomenon is taking place with software: each new product version tends to be more complicated, and contains more code lines by a factor of two or even more. In software technology, increasing code size is created entirely by human programmers. Programmers also take advantage of the component approach: they reuse and modify existing software components and share components among different products. Commercial software components can also be used. Open source software emerged as a side-effect of Internet research. Many commercial products contain open source software. The basic software design process is still difficult to manage and automate, and as a result, software products contain large numbers of defects. They appear to users as low performance, corrupted data and occasional system "crashes." Software professionals have a pet name for the defects they produce: "bugs."

Increasing product complexity seems to be a built-in feature in technology. This can be justified by negative proof: if there were no inherent process of improving technical artifacts by increasing, extending or transferring their features, there would be no technological development at all. We can also argue that the concept of progress is deeply embedded in modern industrial society. It is inherent in the structure of sciences, and the modern man feels quite comfortable attaching the concept of progress with technology, business, society, and even with personal development. On the practical level, companies want to show that their products develop. In a competitive situation, product manufacturers want to assure consumers by offering more features and better performance than competitors.

A special case of product enhancement is that companies have to compete against their own products. They need the consumer to buy their products also in the future, even if they already have a functional product. An often presented example is Microsoft Office. The product does not wear out and in principle, the consumer may transfer the old software to a new computer. As a consequence, new Office versions seem to have ever increasing numbers of new features. As is evident from the Microsoft case, increasing product complexity is not necessarily a blessing for the consumer. It may not be a blessing even for product manufacturers. There is a danger that products become less reliable, more expensive to manufacture, and more difficult to service and repair[6].

We can also distinguish an opposite tendency: product simplification. This becomes necessary, for example, when an innovation is in a mature state, and competition advantage is based on low price. Another motivation to simplify products is to cut quality and maintenance costs. Product simplification can be achieved, for example, by reducing the number of parts, using standard parts and creating integrated designs in which parts perform multiple functions. Often, product functions can be transferred to electronics, which is advantageous because usually electronics and software can accommodate additional functionality without increasing the parts count or product size. For example, in car design, an electronic dashboard can eliminate separate instruments, knobs and levers, an all their assembly components and wiring. In recent years, there has been significant progress in product simplification with copiers, printers and other office machines.

---

[6] A special reason for product complexity is environmental and human compatibility. A combustion engine car has become a serious environmental threat and safety hazard. However, society is currently strongly against abandoning this innovation, so something else has to be done. The basic combustion engine is clearly the most inefficient thermodynamic engine still in wide use. However, economy, pollutant emissions and safety can be controlled to a certain extent with advanced technology. This progress seems to turn the previous manageable automobile into a complicated, delicate and expensive semiautomatic personal transportation system, which requires trained personnel and a special infrastructure for maintenance. As the automobile is not going to disappear in the near future, it will also be an important platform to apply and accommodate new information products, for example, navigation and driver information systems, and leisure applications for passengers.

Information - new commodity

Information is a special commodity. We can see how the development of society has progressed parallel with information processing. The art of writing emerged simultaneously with the magnificent ancient societies of the Middle East. The dissemination of printed books and Johann Gutenberg's improved printing innovations certainly contributed to the breakthrough of scientific thinking and engineering skills. The latest phase of information technology progress is the transition to electronic forms of information. This incredible change took place quite recently: it is less than hundred years since this new information flow, in the form of the telephone, radio, television and recorded music and video started to shape society. We cannot appraise all of its effects: it is too early for a calm historical review, and the process is still going on. We are in the eye of the information tornado, which is continuously increasing in strength and moving to new areas. The overall economical view is fascinating. Efficient industrial production and advanced agricultural technologies can already satisfy human material needs[7]. However, service and information sectors provide unlimited opportunities. Most importantly, information technologies consume only little energy and material resources.

In the case of letters, newspapers and books, the information is coded on to paper sheets, which are then delivered to consumers. The sender of the information needs special technology: a source of paper, and a coding device: pen and ink, or a publishing and printing process. The recipient does not need special technology, but needs to decide what to do with the paper after the information is consumed. There are other information analogies: the theatre as a social information source, and cinema, television, video and music recordings, as means of technology mediated distribution.

It's all digital!

Digitalization is a radical information processing innovation, which simply means that all types of information is converted to numeric form, stored in electronic memories, and processed by electronic calculating devices. This innovation is boosted by the miniaturization of electronics and the application of stored program computers (microprocessors).

---

[7] Here we have to bypass political and macro-economical issues, which are nevertheless not to be disparaged. The control of limited material and energy resources, protection of the environment, and rightful dissemination of the wealth created by industrial production activities are burning questions within societies and on the global scale.

Miniaturization is dependent on the progress of electronics component technology, which has continued for fifty years, and seems to be continuing. The promise of technology is simply that information can be packaged denser and denser, and the cost of storage and processing of information decreases continuously. Actually, the future prospect is not a possible stagnation, but the contrary, another potential and even more radical information revolution due to advances in molecular and nanotechnology and potentially even in quantum physics.

Digitalization has two differing effects on information processing in products: the effect on capacity and the effect on functionality. The capacity of information channels and storage units is limited by technical capabilities and the laws of physics. Digitalization can be used to extend the capacity closer to theoretical limits, which can be considerable. A simple twisted pair wire can carry three to five orders of magnitude more information in digital form, compared to analogue telephone signals. Telephone companies began the digitalization of their trunk lines thirty years ago, for cost savings and efficiency. (Why subscriber lines are still mostly analogue is another, and not simply a technical issue). The same is true for radio and television channels. Using efficient signal coding and data compression methods, the sparse radio frequency bands and cable television networks can transmit several times more data. Digitalization has revitalized radio technology into unforeseen prosperity. At the same time, the World Wide Web pioneered a completely new, interactive and all-digital media.

Concerning capacity we are largely in a favorable position. The digitalization process has not reached its theoretical limits -it is even difficult to imagine where the limits are. For any new application, we either have the information capacity now, or it will become available in some years. However, the effect on functionality, may have interesting qualitative consequences.

Media products

All media products have certain common features. They need some source of information. In addition, there has to be an access and communication infrastructure, so that consumers can utilize the information resource. We may use the term "media application" to denote a media product together with the service it provides.

The information source, or in media research terms, the content, may be visual, textual and voice and it may be on-line, or stored. In private conversations and other social situations, social participation is the main thing, while the content is only a mediator. With information services, the content is the main issue. Most media applications are somewhere between these extremes. We can see that content may be deliberately produced, or a media application may be based on existing content. Sometimes users create the content, like with telephones, discussion groups and live gaming applications. There are currently many existing and established media organizations: television channels, newspapers, film companies, advertisement companies and publishing houses. These organizations produce large amounts of information for established channels. Certainly, new media products also provide new distribution channels and business opportunities, if the media houses are willing to change their way of thinking and operation.

A media product may be a one-way product: a receiver in an information broadcasting application. However, many new products are interactive. The user issues control messages to the sender, or even creates information himself. Most media products require a user interface, and the more interactive the products, the more important is the user interface. It is practically a de-facto standard, that most user interfaces have a display device and a controller (joystick, button panel or keyboard). Voice input and output are currently in limited use.

A media product is often a personal device. So its physical interface and appearance are important. Designers have been trying to image, what kind of things people carry with them, and to use these forms as a basis for new designs. Media product prototypes are designed following familiar forms such as pens, wallets, bags, pendants, eyeglasses and wrist watches. Books and calendars are also suitable prototype forms. If the product is used at home, perhaps also in social settings, it can be compared with furniture.

Next step: smart products

Technology forecasters and corporate strategists wish that they could predict the future and anticipate future products by observing trends, cycles and weak signals. On the other hand, we also know that the future depends on our present actions and choices. One can claim that the present Internet and Web technology were foreseen by persons such as Vannevar Bush and Ted Nelson, but we can also claim that their strong ideas have actually shaped or even created the World Wide Web of today. By observing current trends and by creating a future world through our imagination, we finally create the future and shape it towards our expectations. In the subsequent paragraphs we will discuss some recent ideas and forecasts [17, 18, 28, 39].

The most significant technology trend is associated with the miniaturization of electronics components, and the technology which has been able to exploit the new capability is computer technology - especially in the form of microprocessors. Because the price and size of microprocessors are continuously diminishing, there will be computers everywhere. The words "ubiquitous computing" are often used to describe this situation. As computers become smaller, computer applications are no longer tied to the desktop. Rather, different mobile applications become possible. People carry computers with them, and use them wherever they are. Terms such as mobile computing, nomadic computing and wearable computers describe this phenomenon.

Using computers is not a very natural form of human behavior. Instead of learning complicated procedures and artificial languages, and struggling with clumsy user interfaces, people certainly prefer more direct access to applications. Technology should release its users from the historical limitations of computer usage. The term "context awareness" indicates a situation in which a smart product or application interprets the user situation and provides the user with meaningful options and alternatives. Another related concept is "calm technology:" product technology remains in the background, possibly unnoticed by the user, and reacts only when necessary.

To implement these new ideas and to avoid certain technology drawbacks (e.g., the need for operating power and the physical requirements of user interfaces), the embodiment of the "product" will be reshaped. The product functionality is no longer concentrated in the physical device, which the user carries with him, but it is shared between the user device, and the environment where the application is used. In terms of industrial automation, this concept means instrumentation of the environments where people most often live.

For example, consumers only carry with them some identification device, which allows them to use any private or public media application they wish. This alternative is advantageous, because people then have to carry very little - if anything - with them. Such applications already exist. Distant paragons are cash dispensers and automatic fuelling stations. A similar concept is used in some companies for computer access: there are no personal computer workstations. An employee can go to any terminal and insert his ID card, and his personal workspace is immediately loaded from the company network. Such a concept may be highly economical with workspace computers.

"Augmented reality" is an example of a new content-sensitive service. As people move in an "instrumented" environment, the environment provides additional information, which depends on the user's situation: price and product information for shoppers, navigation information for passers-by, culture and history information for tourists, and so on. The disadvantage may be, that it may be too impersonal for the consumers. People tend to create personal and emotional relationships with the things they use often: a product must be something likable. A partial solution is personalization, or the form through which the consumers perceive the services.

The potential capability of smart products creates completely new applications. Users can access commercial and public information resources, but not only as passive receivers. Interaction has become possible: users provided information for tailoring the products for their personal needs. It is also common, that information, which has been automatically extracted by recording users' behavior and usage patterns is used for personalization of the product, and for new offers and service proposals. A rapidly emerging idea is "social media" and user created content. Users may upload their data content like comments, images and video clips, and they can also share their own personal contents with others. Blogging, YouTube and Wikipedia are well known examples of this new direction of internet service innovations.

New services have potential in homes, but also in mobile form, to facilitate people in their everyday doings at home and outside. A common metaphor is data mining: the possibility to search, structure, extract and combine the resources of service and information providers. Product and service catalogues will become available for users for different applications. Networks can shape commercial, recreational, traveling, educational, social and artistic events. User location services, through satellite or ground based systems, help in guidance and navigation. Public transportation and logistics will be a major application, from improving safety and ease of private driving, to creating of efficient means of public transportation.

Developing these new services is not so much a technical issue. It is a question of social discourse among consumers, service providers and product companies. A proper and flexible infrastructure is clearly needed. There is a need both for secure backbone systems with large coverage, and for local hotspots with advanced and tailored capability.

Application migration

Analogically with computers, smart products are probably more or less multi-functional products. A powerful property of digital technology is that data structures - which may be data products, application programs or communication protocols - can be transformed automatically to be used on different physical platforms. A product does not have to have fixed, built-in functionality. It may adopt the desired behavior and functionality depending on user needs and even automatically according to the situation and location where it is used. Already today a mobile phone can be an instrument of communication, navigation, and payment, and it can run traditional office applications like calendar, spreadsheets and text processing.

Such features are both an opportunity and a threat. There are numerous possibilities for technology misuse, or for unintended consequences. The consumer must have a clear idea, what utility the products offer and how they operate. Trade and services are always based on a contract between the buyer and the seller, and the conditions for making these contracts must remain understandable and safe also in the new and rich technical infrastructure.

User interface

Perhaps the most important technical issue regarding new media products and smart products is the user interface. The present interfaces have adopted a standard form: usually they contain a display device, and some data input and control device. While home applications are flexible, mobile applications are seriously restricted by size and power consumption. New display technologies are emerging, while data input remains a problematic issue. Mobile products cannot easily accommodate a full-size keyboard. Voice input would be natural, but it seems to be the most difficult alternative to implement. Current voice input systems have very limited capability. Limited numeric keyboards combined with interactive soft keys have been successful in mobile telephones. Touch sensitive displays, electric pens, handwriting recognition, and control pads and sticks are also used. More advanced controlling mechanisms have been proposed and experimented with in pilot designs. The user terminal can react to the movements of the hand-held terminal, and to the eye movements and hand or finger gestures. A novel user interface may be based for example on a display device integrated in eyeglasses. The display projects artificial user interface elements in the vision field of the user, who can use his hands or eye movements to operate the application.

In addition to the physical implementation, user interfaces also need the psychological framework, especially some metaphor for visualizing data and data operations. The office desktop was introduced commercially by Xerox about twenty years ago, and it is currently the most popular data processing metaphor. However, the Xerox desktop had interesting predecessors. Since the 1950s, industrial control systems have applied physical metaphors to visualize process information. Data has been embedded on schematic representations of machines and processing systems. Even before computers were in use, control rooms for railway traffic systems, power plants and industrial processes have had their indicators, warning lamps and control levers designed to resemble the symbolic or physical appearance of the systems they represent.

The office desktop is a natural metaphor for office work tasks such as creating and reading documents and drawings, and filing and discarding them. It may not be as useful for more general information related activities. Bookshelves and libraries are also useful metaphors. There have been many attempts to create more general metaphors for human thinking - although, despite intensive scientific research, we still know relatively little of the subject. An advanced concept was introduced by Vannevar Bush already in 1945, in his famous article "As We May Think." The "memex" was a proposal for an electronic information acquisition system. Another interesting proposal was Ted Nelson's "Xanadu." Actually, current Web applications come quite close to these early proposals. Many more or less functional graphical applications are currently in operation on the Web. It is clear that these applications will also migrate to new products. Direct access to existing Internet resources will be one of their main applications.

We may also take a more futuristic approach, through science fiction literature. The Cyberpunk genre became recognized in the 1980s, as Bruce Sterling and William Gibson published their short stories in the "Mirrorshades" anthology. Gibson's technical ideas were largely built around the Internet, which was used as a metaphor of the future information society. Technical capabilities and applications were also extended and projected to the future in an almost prophetic way. Serious researchers on futurology have pointed out on grounds of longtime experience that science fiction literature is not really a source of future technical information, but it can present important viewpoints of the influence of technology on culture and social structure. However, Gibson also presented interesting technical applications. He explained that data structures could be represented by three-dimensional constructs, where users could move as in buildings. He also predicted the emergence of malicious software, which could attack data structures, break into protected areas and even destroy them.

One useful concept is the user profile. Already in present Web applications, users can define profiles, or applications can build user profiles automatically. User profiles provide interesting possibilities, as users can then access the data using their personal priorities, and in continuation, it would also be possible to apply personal and favorite visualization metaphors. Another application of user profiles is that they can represent users to other users. In addition to a name, a profile can be attached to a picture, or even to a three dimensional animated character. William Gibson and other writers have illustrated the use and implications of these artificial characters, which are sometime called "avatars."

Avatars are already in use, in electronic games and animated movies. They have also been demonstrated as representatives of communicating parties in video telephone experiments. Sending moving video images requires a lot of communication capacity. The avatar can be seen as an example of model-based video compression: instead of sending moving images, only model parameters are transmitted. It seems evident that because people are used to communication with other people, avatars have potential for representing both users, and impersonal applications and services. If the use of avatars becomes a standard practice as spokesmen for real people and impersonal services, there will be important ethical and practical issues. Especially, there will be a need for authenticating avatars.

Part II
Inside the companies

Creativity and innovations

Designing is the creation of a new form, regardless of whether we are discussing industrial, engineering or even software design. The issues of creation are both universal and versatile. The word "creativity" is loaded with a number of different meanings and emotional prejudices. Creativity is important element in product development, including the technical part of it. There are a techniques for facilitating and supporting creative work, but a most important and most general creativity aids are natural language and visual representation. We will conclude the chapter by discussing, how organizational and social settings enhance or suppress creativity.

Our presentation of the evolution of engineers' creative status has borrowed its basic theme from Samuel C. Florman [9]. We have described the philosophy behind technical creativity in the terms of Karl Popper [25]. Interesting findings on engineering sociology were reported by Thomas Allen [2]. Cristopher Alexander [1] has illustrated the very nature of all design activities. There is a large volume of creativity literature, presenting similar themes, and we will not name any specific sources. However, we much like Eduard de Bono´s clever term "lateral thinking" [7].

Are engineers really creative?

Engineers have to face a harsh fact regarding their public image. Of all the attributes usually attached to engineering, they do not include creativity. It is certainly agreed upon that in the past, there have been great and creative engineers. Few have not admired Leonardo da Vinci at all - he is referred to often also in this book. Without hesitation we can praise James Watt, Alexander Gustave Eiffel and Thomas Alva Edison. But do we know of any recent heroes? Samuel Florman has pointed out in his book "The Existential Pleasures of Engineering," how the intellectual status of engineering has been drained. After World War II, technology was progressing with increased speed, but the moral background started to decline due to the enormous destruction of the war, the emergence of nuclear weapons, the cold war and global pollution.

Did only the evils of technology cripple the honor and intellectual excellence of a profession? The dark side of technology was well understood in the times when the golden epoch of engineering was emerging. Indeed, already in about 1750 John Smeaton (builder of harbors and magnificent lighthouses) wanted to call himself a "civil engineer" to rid him from being confused with military affairs. Maybe ethical concern is not the reason to consider engineers non-creative. No matter how technology-critical we may be, there is no doubt, that engineering has shaped our human world, especially during the last three centuries. A visit to a modern factory, airport, power plant or hospital will certainly raise admiration towards technical excellence, regardless of what we may think of the creators of those technical marvels.

Evidently, mankind has always felt skepticism and even fear towards technology, which - since ancient Greek - has appeared as a disturbing phenomenon. This theme is visible in many tales and legends, which also illustrate the immoral and distorted character of technologists, and their suspicious or even horrible creations. The stories are usually structured according to the classic dramatic setting from hubris towards nemesis; Prometheus, Daedalos and Icarus, Dr. Jekyll and Mr. Hyde, Golem, Frankenstein's monster, Dr. Strangelove, and as an ultimate example, the biologically degraded technologists, the mean and evil morlochs from the distant future in the dystopia of H.G. Wells, "The Time Machine." However, although so often morally corrupted, the mad engineers and scientists of these stories are ingenious and creative.

One might suspect the existence of professional prejudice. In the past, a considerable amount of serious research about technology and engineering has been conducted by scholars with non-technical backgrounds, for example, from the perspective of philosophy, sociology or economics. To be honest, the common misconceptions that we refer to are rather old. In reality, contemporary technology research is versatile and respected throughout the scientific and technical community. It draws complex and colorful pictures of our modern world, where engineers find familiar features and even themselves. However, everyday knowledge has long roots and considerable inertia. Yesterday's scientific prejudices can still be recognized in everyday thinking and even worse, in general political discourse. Let us consider some common misconceptions.

- Technology is applied science. This theme gives high value to scientists, while technology is only a notorious and non-interesting activity. This theme has several variations. One variation is the so called "linear innovation chain." According to this theory, a successful innovation presupposes a "scientific" idea, which is then refined through laborious but mechanistic procedures into a product. Even our short review of the history of engineering reveals that this conception does not hold true. Science has evolved together with technology, possibly as a consequence of technological development. Modern technology is dependent on the methods of science, but modern science is also dependent on technological apparatus of observation and experimenting.
- Engineering design is the application of technical norms. A technical norm takes the form: "if you want A, and you are in a situation B, you should do X." This is also the form of production systems, which are developed and applied in artificial intelligence research. Several prominent philosophers of technology more or less advocate the claim that the essence of technology is articulated as technical norms. This conception is of course a brutal oversimplification, and if it reflects a common belief, it is most unfortunate with regard to creativity in engineering.

Industrial practices aim for efficiency, standardization and cost efficiency. It is only natural to create and apply standards, rules and norms to save work effort and improve the quality of design solutions. Designers also often justify their design decisions in a norm-like way: "because of this and this, I made that." However, this is really post mortem reasoning[8]. The designer can pick up a satisfying explanation from a set of possible and reasonable norms, but this does not mean that design was guided by the conscious use of a known set of norms. A proof against this proposition is that it is not utilized in practice. Were it true, knowledge management would be a common and everyday industrial practice. Companies would be recording useful norms and including them in design data banks. Against the proposition, managing technical knowledge has appeared exceptionally difficult.

---

[8] Our intention is not to claim that norms do not exist. For example, once a product concept and overall product architecture are defined, usually some effort is made to harmonize the design to be compatible with internal standards regarding product features, implementation components and manufacturing standards. A numbers of norms are applied, inside companies to standardize design practices, and outside in the national or global context, to promote cooperation, and the social and environmental compatibility of products. However, such norms are not necessarily intended to make design easier. Vice versa, often the requirement to take norms into account means hard times for designers.

We can make some concluding remarks. Technological progress, and the irresistible impressiveness, efficiency, beauty and charm of its manifestations leave no room for doubts. Technology is to be regarded as one of mankind's greatest achievements. It is both a material and a cultural achievement. We can admire a technical product such as an airplane without having a clear idea of how the designers of the plane worked together to build it. However, we do have the correct idea that modern designs are created by teams instead of individual virtuosi's. Technological landmarks are now more impressive than ever: we can name diverse applications, including space stations, supercomputers, high-energy physics research facilities and communication networks. We also have more engineers than ever in history. The profession has become too common and familiar to be heroic. If we combine this picture with the misconceptions discussed above, we end up with a caricature of how product teams work: a group of dull, humorless technical clerks going around in their admittedly complicated but mechanical procedures.

Did we miss something? Perhaps the enormous mental gap between the technical wonders and the blunt goblins who create them. Where does the creativity come from? Can it emerge from the mechanistic product development procedures? Can we reveal the secret of these creativity procedures, or could it be that creativity somehow comes from the individuals who take part in the process? After these provocative questions we feel, that we have explained the historical roots for engineers' low intellectual image. Yet, we have not discussed creativity itself.

A creative definition of creativity

It is a common belief that an engineer's common sense is somehow opposite to creativity. Not because engineers are against being creative, but because they do not really know what creativity is or how it works. Engineers are trained in the spirit of Galilean science tradition. They should be able to explain a phenomenon by describing its components and their interactions. However, creativity as a phenomenon seems to escape systematic analysis and examination. Can we do without this word? Indeed, engineers do prefer to talk, for example, about productivity instead of creativity, and they like to be intuitive and even inventive[9]. We can carry out an intellectual experiment - one of the techniques which scientists and engineers often employ. Let us consider that creativity exists in the positive intuitive sense in which it is mostly used, and let us see what follows.

---

[9] The word "engineer" has its roots in Latin and the ancient Rome of the second century, meaning a person who makes clever inventions.

Creativity can be described through the novelty of its products. It is a process, ability or technique for qualitatively generating new solutions for externally or internally posed problems. "Problem" should be understood in a wide context. For example, artists do not solve problems in the usual sense – although a creation of art, be it a picture, story, composition or performance, reveals a new view of reality.

A scientist seems to work with systematic techniques. He wishes to be creative - to reveal and draft a new theory, for example, through applying mathematical or statistical analysis. The procedure itself is not novel; it is well known and well controlled, and it is called "the method" of his school or discipline. However, the scientist needs to be creative in two issues. First he has to invent his research hypothesis. The second issue is to formulate a new theory. To describe scientific creativity, Karl Popper has stated: "... I am inclined to think that scientific discovery is impossible without faith in ideas which are of a purely speculative kind, and sometimes even quite hazy; a faith which is completely unwarranted from the point of view of science, and which to that extent is 'metaphysical'."

A product development engineer is in a worse situation. Given an objective to design a new product, the engineer aims to construct the product, using components and materials that are available, or by defining new components. His work is pure synthesis: he cannot even employ analysis, until he has created something to analyze. The synthesizing process contains intuitive elements, which are difficult to conceptualize or explain. Typical design tasks may have a large number of alternative solutions, and many technical and non-technical constrains. The human ability to create satisfactory designs under such conditions cannot be explained by algorithmic models. Further, the synthesis of systems with qualitatively new emergent properties[10] from elementary system components is another spectacular ability.

To ease the burden of our sample scientist and engineer we have to point out, that they do not work in a vacuum. The scientist works according to his school or discipline and according to the research tradition in his field, and the engineer may use existing technology components and even existing products as a starting point. The degree of creativity also varies. It is measured through novelty: how much the research hypothesis or the new product specification departs from the present and known level. Correspondingly, we talk of radical science and normal science, and with engineering, we talk of radical design and evolutionary design.

We will now attempt to propose a somewhat more accurate description of creative activity and some means to measure it. Defining the unit of measure is easy: it is the novelty of the solved problem, or the novelty

---

[10] Emergent property: a qualitatively new and often unexpected system property, which is created through (often complicated) interactions among system components.

of the solution itself. In a qualitative sense, creativity means solving a problem in a new situation, where no logical or procedural methods can be used. How is this done? We have seen that narratives about creative work procedures tend to utilize deliberately ambiguous and fuzzy words. This indicates that the solution process cannot be described through any tangible terminology or metaphor. Through experience, we know that novel results are produced through those unimaginable procedures. A rational approach is to postulate human ability - creativity - to do the task. This is analogous to the physicists of the 19th century who postulated a medium with unnatural properties - the ether - to explain effects and interactions between physical bodies in an empty space. The postulation was valid and useful until a better explanation was found: the concept of field, and subsequent introduction of quantum physics.

Now we can conclude our intellectual experiment. By postulating a special ability, creativity, we can explain a process, which cannot be observed directly, but which finds its manifestation through novel and tangible products. Still this does not implicate mystification or metaphysical conceptions. Creativity should be understood as a characteristic property and skill shared by all human beings.

Creativity in problem solving

In everyday conversation, creativity is associated with inventions: a sudden and abrupt emergence of a new idea. Often, this idea is a solution to a problem which has plagued the inventor for a long time. This art of creativity might be called problem solving creativity. Literature and history provide stories of great inventions since the time of Pythagoras and Archimedes. Making an invention[11] is apparently a most enjoyable and rewarding intellectual pleasure. According to legends, Pythagoras offered one hundred cows after inventing his theorem, while Archimedes who was taking a bath ran naked into the streets to tell his friends about his invention. The legends are probably not true, but they testify to the commonly recognized joy of inventing. A sudden discovery relieves mental pressure, and also opens new, tempting and yet unexplored visions of reality.

---

[11] We want to clarify our terminology. A novelty is a new thing. An invention is very much like discovering a novelty. An innovation means widespread social, cultural or commercial adoption and application of a new idea. An innovation may be social, or it may be a product. An innovation may be based on an invention, but most inventions do not become innovations. Note that some people also use the term innovation as a synonym for invention.

Many inventors and scientists explain how they suddenly saw the entire problem and the solution space as a flash or X-ray image. However, there are also false alarms - and even memories may be reconstructed. Reality is not black and white. In the world of thought, perceiving and mental simulation boundaries between true and untrue, understanding and misunderstanding are vague and changing. History of science is also a history of false theories such as the unfortunate biological inventions of T. D. Lysenko, or a later debated invention, cold fusion, a few decades later. Patent officers keep receiving patent applications for "innovations" which simply cannot function in physical reality.

A novelty is something which is considered new in the local culture. A novelty is always a social concept. There are no novelties, if nobody is watching. What is well established in one culture, may be totally unknown in another. Social interactions enhance creativity, and this is exactly what is happens when new groups and distant cultures meet. Inventions and innovations may very well be imported. Whether the novelties are invented or imported, they are still novel in their new environment. Of course, an imported novelty is easier to develop into an innovation, as we have already "used a time machine" and seen how it evolves.

So far, we have characterized novelties as if they were somehow substantial and abstract. There are indeed such abstract and distinguished novelties. An abstract novelty may be a law of physics or a new technical principle, which simply have not yet been discovered. For example, an anti-gravity device would be an enormous novelty and invention. The power of this invention comes from two sources. The obvious reason for novelty is that most physicists consider an anti-gravity device impossible. Another precondition is that novelty is culturally recognizable and acceptable. The airplane and the helicopter (inventions that most physicists considered impossible about one hundred years ago) have demonstrated the capability of and need for airborne transport, and science fiction literature has familiarized the public audience with the anti-gravity principle[12].

There are novelties which exist only in a social and cultural context. Many technical innovations are of this form: they deal with social behavioral patterns and habits, which may then be augmented by technology. It is quite possible, that a novelty is not immediately recognized, but gains its value slowly in the course of careful examination and analysis. A familiar example is a scientific novelty such as the theory of relativity. There are also novelties which are not recognized because they are not relevant

---

[12] Indeed, in 1992 a Russian physicist reported, that he had discovered a small reduction of gravity force in an experiment, involving superconductors, magnets and vacuum. The announcement immediately created tremendous media publicity, indicating that there is a high social and economical readiness for anti-gravity based innovations. Regrettably, the gravity effect has been difficult to reproduce.

for the culture. We may have difficulty imagining that the telephone was originally a weak novelty - it was more a curiosity. The telephone turned into a novelty and an innovation gradually after it became familiar and people changed their social habits. The cellular phone advanced much faster because the culture was already familiar with the telephone, and it had only to adapt to mobility. The need for mobility on the other hand was created by another innovation: transportation technology.

So far, we have discussed inventions, but inventing is not necessarily problem solving. A problem usually has an owner. In contrary, it might be difficult to tell who the owner of an invention is. A typical problem in product development is to fit together and balance contradictory product requirements or contradictory implementation alternatives. Each of the conflicting requirements may be considered a sub-problem. It is sometimes possible to solve a critical design issue by making an invention. However, the issue is usually solved by finding a design configuration which is acceptable from the different stakeholders' viewpoints. This means that social, commercial and technical viewpoints have to be balanced.

This may be a challenge for a young engineer, who has throughout his educational history only met problems that only have one correct solution. Another difficulty with design configuration problems is that they have unlimited problem space. Usually, these problems have a large number of conflicting requirements and constraints, which may also have soft boundaries. The problem space becomes enormous, so that there is no practical method of solving the problem analytically. The approach is to solve the design problem through creative and social team work, where the sub-problem owners take part, and which is possibly augmented by technical aids.

Creating form

Another form of creative activity is not really problem solving. An artistic painting, a novel, a symphony from a composer, an aesthetically pleasing house or a microelectronic circuit designed by an engineering team are really not examples of invention or problem solving. They are results of another type of creative work, which is motivated by a need or desire to create a new, complex form. The nature of the working process is quite different. In problem solving or inventing, the solution appears instantly. In form creation, the work is a more continuous, iterative and procedural construction process. However, the creation process may also contain an instant phase, where the general principle of the form structure is revealed. This general form structure is known as the architecture of the solution.

The creation of form has especially been studied in two areas: architecture and writing. A classical work on architecture is Cristopher Alexander's "Notes on the Synthesis of Form" [1]. Alexander makes a note that in modern societies, form creation has been delegated to professionals. As a consequence, new forms appear much faster than in a traditional culture, where design is based on gradual refinements of old forms and self learning. Alexander is especially concerned about the mismatch between user needs and the rapidly created new designs. Why do the design professionals not correct this mismatch? Alexander explains, that even a modest design task is much more complicated than the designers realize. The designers' response to this challenge is to create artificial requirement classification hierarchies for processing requirements. The problem here is that user's needs and wishes do not correspond with the hierarchy, but span over hierarchy levels.

Alexander's proposal to solve this problem is to redefine and develop the design problem into a form in which requirements can be expressed independently, and the expressed design task becomes closer to the technical implementation components. Of course, there is no easy way for implementation. Either the components should be reformulated for closer resemblance to the user's conceptual world, or the users should be more involved in the design process, so that they gradually learn to argue in terms of implementation components. An example of this kind of approach is software application generators, in which the system is defined and assembled using a language and symbol system that are closer to the user's vocabulary.

Writing is another important procedure of design activity. For example, requirements and process descriptions are usually expressed in written language. Analyzing the writing process has revealed that it is not only a mechanical transformation of an idea into readable text. Rather, writing can be considered to stimulate the mental processes of the writer so that the result of the process can be more or less new and even surprising for the writer. This has been observed by recording how the writers' conceptions of the topic change in the course of the writing process.

There are contrasting views about how the writing process stimulates creativity. The discussion distinguishes between the classical and romantic positions. The classical position claims that writing progresses through the generation of a rhetoric argumentation structure. Writing is seen as a goal-directed activity, where the goal is to express the writer's knowledge about the topic. During the construction of the rhetoric structure, the writer may find that the representations of his knowledge contradict, or are not complete for thorough argumentation. The author has to change his argumentation plan, or the communication plan, or acquire new information to create an intellectually satisfactory passage. The romantic position sees that the progress in construction results from spontaneous associations stimulated in the course of text production from original ideas. This theory is supported by findings that not all writers make clear drafts and plans for writing. Their approach is to write to find out what they want or need to say. Apparently, both writer types exist, and the dominant writing style depends on the personality of the writer.

Techniques for augmented creativity

We feel it fair to assume that the secret of efficiency in all commonly applied creativity enhancing techniques is to promote a transition from fruitless pondering into action. A number of special creativity techniques have been proposed, for design and also for other productive work. The apparent popularity of such techniques can largely be explained by the fact that because they tend to organize work processes and promote activity, they always seem to help. If you do not know what to do, do anything!

A straightforward way to support the resolution of design problems is to approach the design task from a system analysis viewpoint. Perhaps it is not quite correct to relate a systematic method with creativity enhancement. Rather, it provides a framework for action and for directing attention. The starting point of the systems approach is to realize, that the problem space (totality of all conditions of the problem and possible elements for solution) is very large – too large for a systematic approach such as a full classification. The only possible solution is then to acquire information on the design problem, conditions and solution candidates in a context-rich form: in natural and visual language. These rich descriptions are then referred to and reconsidered in course of the design process. A supplementary approach is to reconsider the problem statement. A problematic situation is often a conceptual or semantic lock-up. Therefore, the essence of problem solution is to get around the original problem statement.

A very generic creativity enhancement principle is called serendipity[13]. A variation is also referred to as the "garbage can" principle. A common justification of creativity techniques is that invention is hindered by conventional and conservative stereotypes, and the solution is to encourage surprises and unusual combinations. A practical creativity enhancement and invention method is brainstorming, which is by far the most common creativity technique. Many companies apply it frequently. Usually, a

---

[13] An illustrated example of the power of "serendipity" is in the tale of three princes, from "Thousand and One Nights." This is also the original source of the word.

group of 5 to 10 people participate a session, preferably representing different backgrounds, viewpoints and functions. Any form of critique is forbidden, and the goal is to collect as many ideas as possible. The presented ideas are recorded by a secretary, or the participants keep individual notes. Usually, during the first ten minutes of the session, the obvious and banal ideas are recorded. After the banal ideas run out, the novel and reconstructed ideas start to emerge. It is typical that during a 30-45 minute session, more than a hundred ideas are recorded. After the session, the ideas are grouped or classified and a summary is made. Brainstorming is most efficient when it is used for solving a relatively restricted problem, and when the participants have good knowledge of the problem space. Maybe this is why brainstorming is popular in manufacturing and marketing organizations, and only occasionally applied in research laboratories and academic organizations. Several variations of this technique have been developed, and computerized tools are also available.

Eduard De Bono has given several concrete examples of a problem solving technique that he calls "lateral thinking" [7]. This idea also includes the principle of serendipity. Here is the starting point: if a problem has not been solved, it means that conventional approaches simply are not applicable, and the resolution requires some unusual approach. Lateral thinking contains the idea of considering the problem statement from a fresh viewpoint.

Many special techniques, methods and tools have been developed for general and specific use. Even very opposite principles have been proposed: either deliberate stimulation by random associations, or systematic refinement and transformation of problem descriptions. A most original technique has been developed by a Russian engineer Genrich Altshuller, TRIZ. The technique is based on analysis of patent data bases, and it is especially targeted for resolving technical problems and for producing technical inventions.

The traditional design and engineering practices used and evolved over centuries have certainly accumulated collective wisdom about organizing creative work. Another important working technique, which is applied by artists as well as design engineers, is to work with sketches. It has been said, that the most versatile method in engineering is to manipulate visual information to promote the creation of shared understanding. Engineers make sketches while developing the preliminary ideas for a design, they sketch during meetings to promote and exchange ideas within design teams, and they produce disciplined drawings to transfer their designs to prototype shops and production departments. Communication via visual manipulation is also the basic idea of a shared design space, created by visualized computer simulation.

Natural language is also a fundamental tool for creation. We have already discussed how the writing process stimulates creativity. Natural language-based discussions are also an efficient way to promote problem understanding. Natural language is claimed to be inaccurate and prone to misunderstandings. This is true indeed. Special care must be taken, for example, when creating written specifications for requirements and procedures. The benefits of natural language are much more important than its drawbacks. It has been assumed, that universality, transferability and the creative aspects of language are associated with a lack of exactness. The concept of the coherence of discourse is useful for explaining the expressive capability of language. This is a mental capability for making sense on the basis of very incomplete descriptions. A group of sentences in natural language are understood to form a coherent unit, where the referencing elements of sentences are assumed to be pointing at previous items.

Computers have introduced new ways of producing written texts, and provide enhanced methods for accessing and displaying documented information: aids for searching, displaying and editing text, and new document organizing principles. We feel that their effect has been minor. Perhaps the most interesting invention is hypertext, and its big brother, hypermedia. This invention was proposed in its present form by Ted Nelson before computers became common. It is claimed that hypermedia deviates from the artificial, linear text structure and represents information in a manner analogous to the human mind, in the form of a network of associated fragments of information. However, current cognition science does not necessarily support this view. Hypertext lacks the ability to mediate a holistic view, and it has no inherent association capability, which is typical of human thought.

There is also an opposing view. In the worst case, a hypertext document is a collection of uncorrelated fragments of information. The reader of hypertext is in an unfavorable position, as learning the text is not supported by rhetorical structure or coherence. In addition, using these tools is difficult. Creating and managing hypertext systems is tedious and clumsy, requiring a special programming language or an expensive special tool. Engineers cannot draft and play with hypermedia like they do with a pen and paper. Hypertext and hypermedia seem to be technically neutral with respect to creativity. It is clear that they have considerable potential, which requires new kind of tools and platforms - and users need to develop new skills and strategies for reading, searching and manipulating information.

Organizing creativity: individuals, teams and functional groups

Creativity is often considered on an individual and team level. It is true that the individual, personal thinker and actor is the ultimate source of creation. Common wisdom states that a team can be an efficient and productive design unit. It is even said that the performance of a team is more than the sum performance of its members. This may be, but sometimes a team seriously hampers creativity and is a nuisance instead of a facilitator. Instead of continuing with the trendy glorification of team work, we will discuss and elaborate on creative cooperation within a team: can it work, and if so, why? We also want to use a broader perspective, to consider an individual in relation with different social settings.

When we consider creative, mental processes, the world seems to be bipolar: on one side is the individual, and on the other is rest of the world. An individual designer's behavior depends on the environment he is working in, and also on his personality. We begin our consideration with the individual. What is his motivation, and what are the sources of mental energy?

We can illustrate the motivation of an individual in such a way that he is influenced by different forces, see figure 2. Some of the forces are positive and improve motivation, while others are negative. We also distinguish the direction of the forces. External forces are those, which the individual feels affecting his behavior from the outside, while internal forces appear to be born from within. In principle, the organization has at least some control over the forces and can thus improve the motivation of its members. It is interesting, that the polarity of a force is not necessarily clear, but the impact of the force on motivation depends on the situation. For example, a desire to develop a career has a positive motivation effect only, if the organization provides career opportunities. It seems to be a rule that internal forces are more ambivalent than external. For example, the sense of responsibility may lead to faithfulness towards a new idea, or loyalty towards old routines. Internal forces are also difficult to influence.

Of course, external pressure usually causes a reaction, which appears as a change in internal forces, but the direction of the effect may be unpredictable. The dichotomy between internal and external motivation forces apparently distinguishes between two different personality types: those who can be controlled from the outside, and those who are entirely

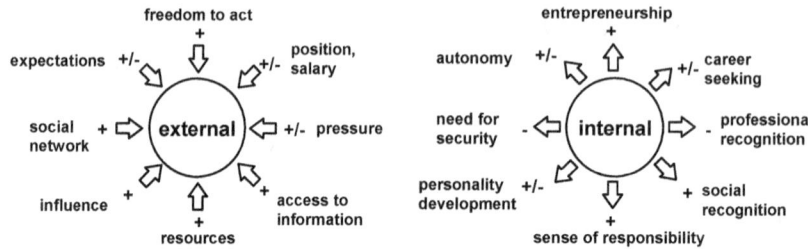

Figure 2. Illustration of internal and external motivation force fields.

internally driven. It is often said that the latter type is more interesting with respect to innovations, but also more difficult to deal with.

We now consider the positive, external forces that act on an individual from the organization theory viewpoint (figure 3). We might call them "creativity enabling forces." We consider four hierarchy levels within the host organization. On the group level, people interact as social beings, and the enabling forces are due to cross fertilization and group dynamics. The next level represents an organizational function. A function develops and provides concentrated resources, for example, tools, equipment and information resources. A network level is created to access resources from outside of the organization. Such resources are extensions of function resources. The final level is the enterprise level, where the main enabling forces are now critical for the entire organization. They are business activities and business opportunities.

So far, we have discussed organizational levels from the individual to the enterprise. We also want to present another viewpoint. Social networks are important for individuals, and they penetrate all other organization levels. Thomas Allen has performed outstanding sociological studies within engineering communities [2]. He noticed that there are always two different organizational mechanisms. There is the official structure, which in a modern organization can include functional groups, projects and teams. Then there is the unofficial network of social relations. The social network does not map directly to the official structure, but it crosses boundaries. Allen's special interest was to study communication. He discovered that information flow follows the social network. When he studied the intensiveness of communication, he noticed that communication was not even. It concentrated on certain network nodes. Allen named these individuals "gatekeepers" because they obviously acted as important information sources. It was also significant that the gatekeepers were usually not team or group leaders.

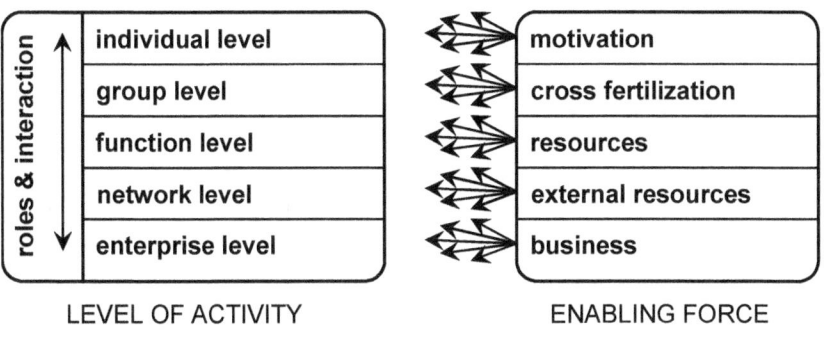

individual level	motivation
group level	cross fertilization
function level	resources
network level	external resources
enterprise level	business

LEVEL OF ACTIVITY   ENABLING FORCE

Figure 3. Enabling forces on different levels of organization.

A penetrating finding was that regarding communication, the social network is always more important than the official structure. He also made other important findings. When he compared low-performing teams with high-performers, he noticed that most productive teams were part of social networks, which extended outside functional groups.

Allen's classic work, although performed more than twenty years ago, is still illuminating. The modern communication network, in the form of electronic mail and the Internet is more advanced. However, its significance is difficult to evaluate: when Allen studied the use of external information, he found it less important. On the other hand, he found social relations which extended beyond functional groups valuable.

Regarding team work, at least two conclusions can be made. First, setting up design teams should not impede social networks. There are some possibilities to comply with this principle. Teams may be based on personal interest and curiosity. The principle of information transparency aims to provide maximum visibility for design information. This principle prevents less active network members to block information from others. The second lesson is that diversity of information nourishes team creativity. Multi-disciplinary design teams are thus strongly encouraged.

Managing knowledge

A familiar proverb is "Knowledge is power". "To know" means "to know how to." Knowledge is intermixed with the intention of doing something. It is closely related with action. Knowledge is applied in action, and knowledge is created and acquired from action. Knowledge is comprehensible and practical, and at the same time, it is difficult to grasp. We cannot really encode knowledge into documents and databases. The nature of knowledge has been illuminated through the metaphor of bicycling. It is possible to write formal instructions for bicycle riding: The driver sits in the saddle, he creates movement by rotating the pedals with his feet, and controls direction by turning the handlebars towards the direction he wants to go[14]. However, this information is useless, if someone really wants to learn how to ride a bicycle. The only working method is to try and practice it with a real bicycle. Once somebody has learned it, he still cannot explain it.

Knowledge is related to action. Let us stop to take a breath. We should not be confused because of inaccurate wording. For example, sometimes people talk about scientific knowledge. Their purpose is to say that scientists know things about the laws of nature. However, this knowledge is not for action, but rather of an analytic and static nature. It is for explaining nature, as our theory was for explaining bicycling. To

---

[14] As often happens with theories, this intuitive riding theory is erroneous. Actually, the rider uses the handlebars, not to control direction, but to control his balance. The direction is controlled indirectly through balance control, by moving the direction of gravity force off the trajectory of movement. For example, to initiate a turn to the right, the driver first turns the handlebars to the left, to get him off balance. He then re-balances himself by creating a right-turning trajectory by carefully turning the handlebars back to the right, so that the centrifugal force and the horizontal component of the gravitational reaction force balance each other. Unfortunately, not event this improved theory makes it easier to learn to ride a bicycle.

avoid confusion, it is common to distinguish between silent (or tacit) knowledge and articulated knowledge (codified information such as documents).

How do engineers and designers know how to design? How is it managed, learned, shared with others and facilitated? To approach this issue, we first need to discuss some fundamental principles, and to clarify the nature of technical information and knowledge. What is the secret of the human capability of creating novel, complicated, useful and aesthetically pleasing artifacts? We have discussed creativity, and now we have discovered knowledge. Which one is the explanation? Clearly both elements are necessary. Whatever resources are available: information, e.g., knowledge and technical instruments, they can be utilized in a creative way. It can be put another way: if there is a lack of information and knowledge, creativity has no wings.

Innovation process is a play among stakeholders in our technical society, especially between producers and consumers. In the course of this social discourse, the participants develop a shared understanding and vocabulary about technological instruments and their application opportunities. The accumulation of technological knowledge is not restricted to the engineering community, and is a much larger concept. Discussing knowledge requires the introduction of a number of concepts and terms, which are not used in everyday technical discussion.

Michael Polanyi [24] has elaborated the concept of tacit knowledge, Nonaka and Takeuchi [19] have demonstrated the importance of knowledge for organizations, and Vincenti [32] has given a rich picture of engineering knowledge in the field of aerodynamics. Karl Popper [25] and Herbert A. Simon [27] provide a philosophical contribution to understanding the artificial. Another important information category is design rationale (Moran and Carrol [16]). Thomas Allen [2] has made interesting sociological findings about engineering work.

Special character of artificial things

Technology is the most human phenomenon on earth. Animals do not have technology in the same sense, although they control their environment and produce artifacts, for example, by building nests. However, animals do it by instinct. Animal technology is tied to animal biology, and evolves slowly as the species evolves, while human technology, as we all know, is extremely dynamic. Is technology a living or autonomous thing, as it is often referred to? It is a common dichotomy to consider nature being made up of living beings and lifeless things. However, this dichotomy is insufficient, when considering human made artifacts. Scissors are a lifeless object, until they are in a human hand. Together they are much more capable than each of them alone. Another example: a book is a bundle of meaningless paper sheets, sprinkled with strange patterns of ink. It remains this way if there is no one to read it!

To highlight the significance of the subjective presence of human intellect, Popper and Eccles have proposed three world categories (figure 4). Before all, there has to be the physical world, containing both living beings and lifeless things. If we elaborate the physical world , we notice that it also has to include invisible things, which we cannot observe with our senses. According to general understanding of physics, we know that the invisible things are also real and they really do exist: fields, elementary particles, the laws of nature, etc.

The second "world" is quite different: it is inside our heads, what we feel and experience. It can be called the self; subjective existence. It consists of experiences, mental states, self and conscious thinking. Although its content is difficult to express in exact terms, the world no doubt exists. There is a connection between these worlds. It is commonly understood that our subjective existence is a result of material processes. We also know that objects and activities of the material world are the causes of many subjective experiences. On the other hand, through intention and action we can produce effects on the real word things. Actually, we do it all the time.

Third of these realms is the ma-made world: it may be called the world of the artificial. It contains artificial objects, which have a cultural and social character. This character is the significance of the objects, which is created by subjective interpretation. Artificial objects may be material: artwork, books, tools, machines, furniture, etc. There are also immaterial

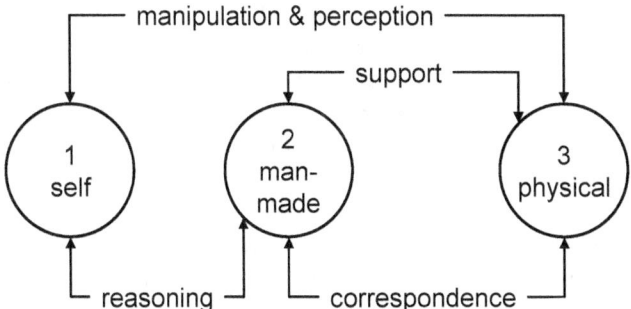

Figure 4. Three worlds, according to ideas of Popper and Eccles.

artifacts, such as scientific theories, languages, and stories. To illustrate this category, we can consider a story, which is imagined by some person. The story is an artificial creation, but it is also supported by the subjective experience, and is only accessible by the storyteller. Of course, it is also supported by the physical existence of the human body. The story can then be told to other people utilizing the vibrations of air as media. The time span of this physical form of the story is, however, very limited. The story may also be written on paper and bound into a book. Now, it has become a physical object with a reasonable stability and life span. At the same time, it is definitely an artificial object, because it certainly is something much more than a bundle of paper with ink patterns, at least as long as there is someone who can read it.

The three world model can be used to illustrate the character of technology. It is easy to see that technology belongs the artificial world. Technology is essentially dependent on knowledge: there has to be someone to know how to deal with it. If knowledge is not present, technology is reduced to a collection of non-functional physical objects, and the cultural part of it is muted: it is reduced to a pure physical object without any significance.

Other peculiar characteristics of the artificial are discussed in a small but influential booklet by the Nobel laureate Herbert A. Simon. Simon is concerned about the human ability to understand and manage artificial things. Most modern products are complicated. They consist of different parts, which interact with each other. As the parts may have several possible ways to function and communicate, the number of possible interactions becomes much too large to be explored or understood for example by a design team. The boundary between the artificial thing and the environment is especially critical because the environment's effects upon the artifact are not bound: In the various situations in which the artifact is in contact with the environment, the environment may produce an unlimited number and sequences of effects on the artifact.

As a result, in real situations, the artificial thing exhibits a number of behavioral patterns and tendencies which emerge due these interactions. These behaviors and tendencies are called emergent properties. Some emergent properties are designed in to the artifact on purpose, but most of them are side products.

Emergent properties may be aggregates of large number of product elements and properties. Thus, they may be difficult to understand and control. Vincenti illustrates this by analyzing an important example: an aircraft's flying qualities. Flying qualities are difficult to quantify. The opinion of desirable properties depends on the pilot's experience and on the task of flying an airplane. Flying qualities are also related with other emergent properties such as stability, safety, passenger comfort and operating economy. In purely technical terms, they emerge from aerodynamic design, engine design, and the design of controls and the cockpit. These dependency functions are difficult to quantify. Despite many obstacles, it is important to apprise and manage flying qualities. In practice, this property is managed through test fights and experience. That is, by employing accumulated knowledge.

Some emergent properties are important, some useful, some are meaningless or irritating, and some harmful. Extreme examples of unwanted emergent properties are the effect of DDT on higher animals, including man, and the most dramatic consequences of the reaction dynamics of graphite moderated nuclear reactors, as demonstrated by the reactor accident in Tshernobyl. Simon's concern is both justified and continuously relevant. The unwanted effects of technical artifacts are mitigated by the fact that most technical innovations develop through gradual refinement and by improving earlier designs, giving time to create culturally shared knowledge about dealing with an invention. We have already pointed out how radical innovations are unpredictable and susceptible to failure. However, radical and rapidly evolving innovations can also have surprising and not always pleasant consequences.

The functionality of artificial things depends on knowledge. Knowledge about technical things is about using them, and also about creating and maintaining them. This shared knowledge can be referred to as technical culture. On the other hand, culture is not uniform. There are different cultures in different countries, and sub-cultures within countries. The culture[15] of product engineers is also different than that of consumers in general. When a new product is introduced to consumers, it is not necessarily a question of whether they like it or not, or even of whether they need it. It may be that they just do not understand it. If there is not enough understanding, the product's possibilities and perspectives are not seen: it is merely a surface, empty and indifferent.

Nature of technical knowledge

For about a thousand years, weapon smiths in the Middle East, China, Persia and India have known how to make high-quality swords. They were lightweight, had excellent durability and flexibility, and could be made very sharp. In Europe, the material for these swords was known as Damascus steel. The blade of a finished Damascus sword has a characteristic pattern of fine figures, the so-called damask pattern. The pattern was not for decoration, but reflected the technical secret of the sword: a super

---

[15] In everyday discussion, culture is often understood hierarchically, as a collection of appreciated achievements. In sociological research, culture is a central concept, meaning a collective subjectivity; a shared way of living, acting, perceiving the world and meanings.

high-carbon steel alloy called "wootz"[16]. The material is not homogenous, but contains visible domains of carbide and residual carbon, processed into a certain structure and orientation. The detailed manufacturing process was akin to a military secret, which was maintained in the workshops as a professional tradition. Sword making was dependent on very specific raw materials, tools and equipment. The entire manufacturing procedure was sensitive, from producing the high-carbon ingots with small amounts of other additives, through many cycles of forging and heat processing to finishing the blade. Because the original art was created over long periods of time, it could only be adopted in one man's lifetime through practicing in a master's workshop. Sword making was indeed an extreme example of a knowledge-dependent technology. So much so that the art of producing wootz for Damascus steel swords was lost in the 18th century and despite many attempts could not be revitalized. Only recently has modern science revealed the secrets of the material through spectral analysis and electron microscopy, and wootz metal is again available.

This example illustrates how generally available literary information, and even existing and fully representative product samples may be insufficient for reverse engineering the design and manufacturing procedure. Information had to be supplemented with personal knowledge. A similar situation still exists in product development today. Modern products are so complicated that it is not possible to document or collect documents and data files that would provide a complete description of its design and manufacturing. Technical information is always incomplete and insufficient, and the missing pieces are covered through knowledge and culture. Knowledge and information are not the same thing. In product development, they are in a constant, cyclic and mutual interaction process, which is described so well by Nonaka and Takeuchi. Information will turn into knowledge during a personal and social learning process, and knowledge on the other hand turns into information in the course of organized working processes (figure 5). It is a continuous dialogue between internal, tacit representation, and articulated, external forms. Activity and social setting are the catalyzing elements in this process. The need to communicate with others causes the urge to express individual ideas, using language and images. Observing what other participants express, and interpreting and organizing this information, stimulates personal learning.

---

[16] Knives and swords made of thin welded layers of steel of different carbon content have been continuously produced and often referred to as Damascus steel products. Although they are highly decorative, their performance is not comparable with "wootz" products.

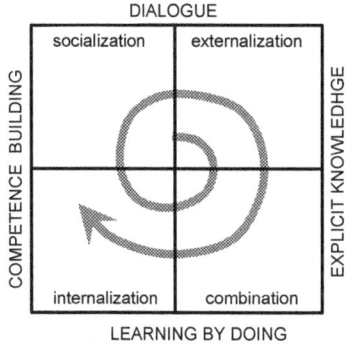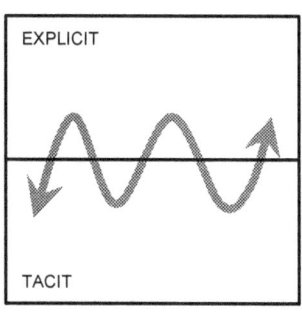

Figure 5. Information-knowledge transformation on individual level and in organizational setting, according to Nonaka&Takeuchi.

The interesting and important remark by Nonaka and his colleagues is that the extent of knowledge creation is determined by the community participating in the process. If product knowledge creation is limited within a company, the knowledge remains localized, and customer's voice is dependent on some limited and deliberate channel. If partners in the value chain, including customers, are involved, the knowledge cycle supports building a network. Within a company, the outcome of the product knowledge process is the ability to manage the product in the technical sense. When the entire value chain is involved, the knowledge process helps to create the infrastructure, as well as the cultural adoption of technology.

Incompleteness of technical information

The output of a product creation process is a planned set of design and product data, which will accurately describe the final product and introduce it to the manufacturing and distributing processes. This sounds simple, and to explore technical information a little further, it is only necessary to provide some kind of classification for it. Before we can go this far, we have to make one reservation. All technical information is actually set up as a collection of models of reality.

System sciences, or more actually, the general failure of system sciences has demonstrated the enormous versatility and complexity of the real world. No model can approach this reality, so any model is a practical simplification. Models which are basic elements in the product industry have to be very practical and efficient. This means that they are necessarily incomplete. We have discussed knowledge because it is the way to cross the cleft. Any product document is incomprehensible without proper knowledge, as if it were in some foreign language.

There are actually two kinds of incompleteness. The first is related with private and public cultures. On the local level, within a company, people refer to internal practices and conventions of dealing with their technology. It is not necessary to describe or design everything, because there are always available people and teams who can perform critical activities. On the public side, outside of the company, there is a general social and cultural awareness of technology and its applications. It has been created through common and professional education, and by the everyday presence of technology. For example, when the cellular phone was introduced to the public, it was not necessary to explain how to make a call or dial a number. The cellular phone had adopted the conventions and practices developed for automatic telephone networks.

The second reason for incompleteness is that technology is composed of existing modules and components, which are merely referred to by identifying them and describing the interfaces and interconnections between the components. A considerable amount of information is embedded in components, machines, materials and processes in the techno-cultural environment. The continuous physical presence of artifacts is necessary to maintain and develop a culture with technical knowledge: it is required in the companies producing the artifacts, but also for entire technical societies.

Ontological and procedural forms of technical information

We will now take a closer look at technical information. Its aim is to support and maintain the creation of technical artifacts. For this purpose, two basic types of information are needed. Ontological information aims to answer the question "what is it?" It explains the nature of technical things: their structure, properties and behaviors. Ontological information can be found in the public domain: in engineering textbooks, advertisements and product specifications. Design documents are usually a private and confidential ontological information: they explain product architecture, its composition of parts and modules, details of self-made parts, programs for microprocessors, performance specifications, and the results of product and module tests.

Procedural information aims to answer the question "how?" How is the product used in different situations, and how is it managed in the companies producing it. It is information about manufacturing, as well as about operation, maintenance, and disposal or recycling. A visible part of procedural information are manuals and instructions. Such documents are necessary for reference and internal standardization, but insufficient for creating the actual procedures. Here we meet with what Nonaka and Takeuchi refer to as collective knowledge. In forming collective knowledge, a shared culture emerges, which is distinguished as local folklore and narratives. The knowledge is also hard-coded in the structure of organizations, as operating processes. The manuals and instructions act as reference, but the actual processes are made up of behavioral patterns of process participants, and the patterns are learned during the knowledge formation process.

A special and important type of ontological information is design rationale. It is a justification for the design of artifacts: why it is the way it is. It is needed to maintain the product and to transfer product information. Design rationale is discussed and processed during product design, in design team meetings and technical review meetings. It is the most important discussion topic during the design phase. Design rationale is documented as meeting memos, design drafts and e-mail messages. It is highly product and situation specific; actually, it is an integral part of the design process.

Most of this information is discarded when the design is completed: it is only occasionally documented as design justification documentation. Considering the improvement of the product design process, capturing the design rationale is a potential possibility, but also a challenge.

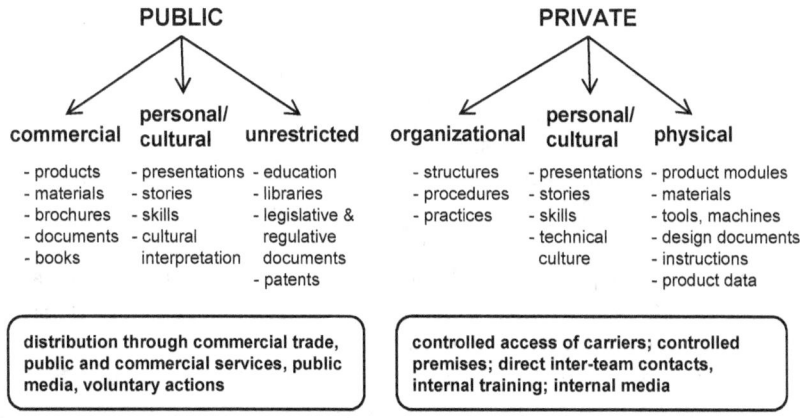

Figure 6. Technical information: public and private domains.

Technical things themselves are an important information source. Much can be learned and understood by playing around with technology. Hands-on work with technology is essential for thorough understanding and management. Embedded information cab also be extracted through systematic reverse engineering.

Information in data records and documents

An important class of technical information is produced on purpose, or is generated as a by-product of some technical process. Information may exist in a human-readable form. Such information is called documentation. Information can also be machine readable - or machine readable files can be made comprehensible to humans. Software program code is intended to be interpreted by computers, but it is as important for software designers to be able to read it. Three-dimensional design data are intended to be displayed to designers and other technical persons, but cannot be understood without special programs. Thus, the 3-D files are used as input for computers, for example, for rendering realistic visual models, or to be converted into finite element models for structural analysis.

Technical documents are always created for some specific purpose. They are used to support the design process, and to support the product in different phases of its life cycle. There are various needs and reasons for technical documentation:

☐ Documents serve as manufacturing templates. This is the ordinary purpose of design documents. In earlier times, it has been a practice that drafts and drawings, often called "control drawings" have been used to communicate with the prototype workshop. When the prototype is satisfactory, the detailed manufacturing documents, engineering drawings, are then made, as a reference for production. Usually, a prototype requires alteration in many ways to make it suitable for production, and there is a risk that the changes are not back-propagated to engineering drawings.

☐ Documents provide intellectual platforms. Engineers use drafts, drawings and notes to support the constructive design process and to share ideas with other design team members. This is also an ancient form of documentation. Intermediate documents of various types are important creativity enhancement tools. Most design phase documents are discarded after the product is finalized. However, a selected set of design material is archived, to be used for product updates, and to support the design of subsequent, new product models.

- Analysis and simulation templates are needed to support the design of product details. Modern technology applies scientific methods. Design and implementation solutions are verified during the design process, often even before prototypes are built. The basic idea is to build a mathematical model which corresponds with the part of design to be verified. Model equations are formulated, and calculations are made to calculate theoretical properties of the item. A derivative technique is computer simulation, where more complex situations can be investigated using approximate numeric methods. A typical simulation example is finite element calculation, which is applicable for a number of problems: determination of strength, temperature distribution, and flow of gases or liquids.

- Explanatory technical documentation is intended to guide the people who deal with the product in different phases of its life cycle. Technical manuals are created for maintenance personnel, system integrators, validation activities, training and end users. Technical presentation material is needed for sales support. A special type of explanatory technical documents is design rationales, which are created and used during the design process, to support design teams and design management. Design rationales are also useful for supporting designers of new product models.

- Management documents are needed to manage product related processes, but also the products themselves. Process management documents are different plans, for projects and their tasks and phases. A plan includes, e.g., objectives, the schedule, a task list and a resource list. Reviews, inspections and tests are based on plans, and produces minutes and records. Product management aims to control the properties of a product, using techniques such as quality control and product assurance. Product management also involves procedures, plans and records.

Scientific touch in modern engineering

If we consider the work of technical professionals as a black box, it essentially seems to be manipulation of technical information. A closer look reveals that this manipulation is as much the creation of knowledge as it is creating information recordings. In the actual working situation, we refer to the phase of Nonaka's knowledge cycle in which information turns into a collective form of knowledge: a shared culture, and organizational and social structures. We will conclude our discussion on engineering knowledge with a discussion about how it is created in organizational settings.

We need to refer to another typical modern profession: the scientists, because science is definitely involved with modern technology. So far, we have deliberately avoided of referring to science and scientific information, although the power of modern technology is very much in the application of scientific methods. We will now discuss what this scientific touch means in practice.

An important scientific method is experimental work, in which prototypes and their parts are investigated under controlled laboratory conditions. A controlled environment and careful quantified measurements are necessary to prevent the effect of external disturbances, to allow comparing experiments, and to be able to repeat them if necessary. Experimenting is referred to as testing, and it is used to verify the technical functionality of design and implementation solutions.

Another application of scientific methods is working with theories and models. Here, engineers apply mathematics and the overall methodology of physics. There are also technical sciences, which are derived from "pure" physics; for example, strength analysis, fluid and gas dynamics, thermodynamics, circuit theory and telecommunication theories. Although engineers "just apply" physical and mathematical theories, there is one considerable difficulty. Fundamental physical theories assume a free space, while in technical application the physical effects take place in a closed volume [32]. Applied models have to take into account boundary conditions. Actually, a tailored model has to be constructed for every application case. A commonly used computer supported analysis tool for field problems within a bounded volume is finite element modeling (FEM). Because this kind of modeling is difficult and time consuming, analytical verification is often omitted, and the design solution is based on judgment by analogy, tradition and earlier experience. The solution is then verified through extensive prototype testing.

It is evident that engineers have to work like scientist when analyzing and exploring their designs. It is also true that scientists work like engineers when they plan and implement their experimental apparatus. However, the basic working patterns of scientists and engineers are strikingly different, since the objective of a scientist is to gain information: a new abstract theory, while the objective of an engineer is to create a new technical artifact or a new process. Thomas Allen has performed comprehensive sociological studies about the working patterns of scientists and engineers. As a conclusion Allen sees engineering work as conceptually different to scientific work. Allen makes a strict distinction between engineering and scientific work, although he points out that certain fields of technology, for example, electronics, are more closely related to the frontier of science than, say, mechanical design.

Allen makes an important remark on the use of information. Both technology and science are dependent on external information, which is encoded in written form. Science transforms this information into new written documents. Technology on the other hand, encodes this information in a physical form: technology produces physically existing technical artifacts. This encoding process is partially reversible. Technical artifacts carry identifiable information about the production process, and the underlying technical and scientific principles. This information can be extracted through a process called reverse engineering. Reverse engineering is an important, although also controversial industrial practice. Although Allen admits that freely available technical goods, as well as competitors' designs, are frequently analyzed to examine their structure and principles of operation, apparently he does not see this form of information as being significant.

In his sociological study, Allen looked especially at communication patterns among engineers. Usually, engineers are working in rigid functionally arranged or project organizations. These organizations tend to exclude engineers from external communication, by requiring that the work is focused on the problems imposed by the organization, and especially when working with new designs, to keep the work secret from outsiders. As a consequence, communication patterns among engineers are localized and narrowed. Allen also found that within a functional group, contact patterns accumulated on certain persons, and the same persons also communicated intensively outside the group. Allen called these persons gatekeepers. The function of gatekeepers appears to be the translation of external information into a form that can be utilized by the organization. On the other hand, Allen and his colleagues could not find gatekeepers in basic scientific research. His conclusion was that gatekeepers are needed because of the local nature of technology. In basic science, there is no use for gatekeepers because scientists do not need to translate anything. The language of science is universal among scientists, and they communicate freely over organizational boundaries. Information transfer for technology is based more on direct contacts. Allen considers the transfer of people to be the most efficient means of technology transfer between organizations.

Allen also makes a note that the so-called technical sciences resemble their non-technical counterparts. Thus, it is natural that engineering education addresses analytical sciences. However, although most of the engineering education is analysis oriented, the actual nature of engineering work is entirely different, which is paradoxical. Learning design skills and industrial practices takes place mainly at workplaces and as professional training. Herbert A. Simon has also been concerned about this education gap, as is evident in his search for "sciences of the artificial." Since the classical works of Allen and Simon, there has been some progress in the teaching programs of universities and engineering schools. Still, the academic world has been slow to react to technical progress and social change, which during the last decades, have originated from industrial research and development laboratories.

It has been said that science encodes information in a textual form and technology in physical form. However, this statement is incomplete. Language-based technical documents, which are an extension of human linguistic capabilities, are essential elements within the technology creation process. Additionally, working with visual representations or artificial symbolic languages, probably has similar creative functions. We have described documents essentially as reference storage, and for communicating of technical matters. However, as Allen's studies have demonstrated, technical documents are not universal, but understandable only in the social and cultural context. We summaries the information view of the design process as follows. Design is an activity bound to the local environment and culture. This culture is created through coordinated activity, during discussions within a design team, and between the design team and the user community.

This discussion can benefit from a communication space, in which participants of the design process can exchange and simulate their ideas through visual and textual messages. One part of the activity is access to design documents. Documents support the discussion, and they are also created in the course of the discussion.

Navigating corporate information resources

The modern industry is information intensive. There is a common understanding that technology development, as well as the competitiveness of technology companies depends especially on local information resources, and on personal and social knowledge. We have also discussed how the coded, documented information is in continuous dialogue with knowledge, and how these resources evolve in the course of this dialogue. The coded information is entirely in electronic form, which provides potential technical possibilities to support and facilitate the utilization of this information. We will now investigate how companies collect and disseminate the coded forms of information.

Universal versus application-bounded data

The value of information as an asset and resource has been recognized a long time ago, and since the increasing industrial application of computers in the 1960s, there has been a vision, that computers can greatly accelerate the information revolution. An individual expert has a considerable amount of professional information and experience. The human memory has a remarkable capacity, and it is especially efficient in recalling information according to any aspect of the content. However, the human memory also has some drawbacks. It is inaccurate and unreliable, and the learning process is slow and tedious. Visionaries have dreamed about a combination, where a specialist could have immediate and fast access to an electronic collection of data, augmented by some efficient access method. A library is the traditional model for information collections, and information scientists and librarians have been working on information access methods for centuries.

A combination in which a skilful specialist could empower his work with a fast electronic information access system would be fantastic. Expressions of this dream can be found in science fiction literature, and serious professionals have made interesting proposals. Vannevar Bush presented his "memex" concept when computers were still incapable of supporting such systems. However, computers have advanced. Today, public libraries operate electronic, on-line search databases, although the collections are still off-line. The World Wide Web has created a global electronic data repository, which links numerous libraries and even more numerous other data sources with efficient search engines. Many companies utilize Web technology in their internal data networks, intranets. It is commonly agreed upon that working with external information is much more efficient than, for example, 20 years ago. A shade of disappointment can also be detected. While computers, networks and databases offer their users enormous amounts of data, they still cannot digest the data. It is up to the user to find out the real value of the data that computers provide.

While the library analogue is one example of electronic information systems, computer-based information provision has also found other routes. We have pointed out, that information is usually used for a specific purpose. Both knowledge and information are activity specific. In professional and industrial use, the most successful information systems are targeted on some special application. The early successful computer applications usually processed large numbers of relatively simple data objects with a standard form: population registers, customer registers, bank accounts, telephone catalogues, product catalogues and so on.

Later, several tools for word processing, planning and different design arts were developed. Although computer-based tools created electronic documents, the tools themselves possessed very limited capabilities for managing the documents. Typically, the documents have been printed on paper, and then managed and filed manually. Evolution and the adoption of document management and retrieval applications has been sluggish. Among the first applications were depositories and version control applications for computer programs and document management systems.

Today, dominant computer architecture is based on local area networks, which integrate computers and user workstations. In this environment, it is possible to share data files, by using shared computer disks, and creating HTML pages with links to shared files. Such arrangements are common. However, they are relatively inefficient, as data access is based on external knowledge about the location of files. Thus, these systems are only electronic analogies of traditional file cabinets. The hyperlink approach is slightly better, but creating and maintaining the link system requires a lot of work, and this kind of arrangement is feasible only for relatively passive data: for example, for work instructions and quality system documentation.

In search of product and design information

We will now consider what kind of information resources companies, and how they are related with product design activities.

☐ Databases for resource management and cost control:
   Companies have databases, which support commercial activities and accounting. They deal with concepts such as cost and working hours. Such data is useful for tracking the efficiency of departments. It is important to know the overall economical figures of product development and product profitability, and even product development projects can benefit from cost accounting.

☐ Message systems:
   Everyday activities in companies consist of a large number of meetings, which generate short memorandums and notes. Messages are also generated as part of activity processes, and spontaneously. Databases can be established to keep track of these messages, for example, messages can be arranged according to topics, dates and categories. Usually, such systems include an integrated e-mail system. An e-mail system without a database for messages is, however, rather inefficient, as keeping track of messages is the responsibility of the users. A message database is well suited to recording design team and project meeting minutes, review reports, test reports and other similar material. Thus, team members can record project history and discussions in the course of the design effort in a form which enables sharing ideas and later recollection.

☐ Product data management systems:
   Dedicated systems for managing product data, PDM systems, are established especially in production oriented companies. Their primary purpose is to keep track of all the components and materials needed for production and to support their purchasing and storage - the storage of finished products is also supported. The system is based on product part lists and product configurations. It may also contain documents needed for production such as engineering drawings and machine control files. When a product is designed and released for production, product data is generated based on design data.

☐ Document management systems:
   An electronic system for storing of any type of information. Rather

than physical location, document retrieval is based on logical information. For this purpose, documents have to be tagged with auxiliary search information. This is either generated by the document author, or automatically according to document content or by the context where it is created. Document management systems allow the creation of efficient data archives for design data. For example, documents can be tagged with a product identifier, document type, part type, document release status, project and task identifier and so on. The use of document management systems is not a common practice in product design, but it is useful and has potential. If a document management system is combined with a system for project or workflow control, document tagging can be more or less automatic.

☐ Specific design environments and tools:
Dedicated computer supported working environments for product design can be established using commercial system products or developing proprietary systems. These systems contain some kind of process support, which implements a general product design model, the so-called systems engineering model. The advantage of such a system is that it automatically collects and tags design documents belonging to a certain project. Commercial design environments usually cover only a part of the design process, the software process is typically excluded. Proprietary design support systems are expensive to develop. They are used in large-scale industry, for example, in airplane design. Especially with proprietary systems, specialized design support tools can be integrated with the design environment.

☐ Software development environments:
Being a class of design environments, software tools support different tasks and phases in software development: code writing or generation, compiling and system building, analysis and testing. These tools may contain, or even be built around a modeling tool. Software designers often employ a configuration management system, to keep track on different variants of produced modules, and to control module release and module changes. Version management systems resemble document management systems, but are developed specially for controlling of software files.

☐ Requirements engineering:
This tool class represents general purpose analysis tools. An example are tools for managing product requirements and product consistency. They provide a very specific form for design information management. The tools keep track of dependencies between product modules and requirements. If a requirement changes, it is possible to find out which modules need to be updated. If a module is changed, the tool indicates the modules and requirements that are influenced.

There are also tools for analyzing product concepts: for example quality function deployment (QFD) tools.

□ Project management:
It is advantageous to organize product development into projects, and project management software can be used as additional support. Project management systems usually contain some amount of product related information: they contain information on tasks, their scheduling and status, and resource allocation information. In principle, it would be useful to include control, and even design documents with project management information, although most common product management systems do not support this.

□ Corporate intranet platforms:
A straightforward approach to create a corporate intranet is based on a local area network, which interconnects computers and user workstations. Access to data is based on network paths and file specific names, and file link catalogues are often maintained on web pages. Although such a network is easy to establish, it has limited functionality and it is difficult to maintain. To improve operation, commercial and proprietary intranet platforms have document management and workflow control functions and web style search engines. Such an environment allows efficient management of design documents, for design time communication and to create a store for sharing information with different users, to be reused on later designs and to support other product related activities.

Information and knowledge in action

The evolution of computer-based information systems indicates how closely information is related to activity. It is difficult to distinguish between "pure data" and "application software." Special applications actually contain embedded knowledge and instructions for their users, so that an efficient and well designed application greatly enhances the "data" it uses.

Although modern organizations contain and use large amounts of electronic information, the exploration and assessment of this information is not easy. In addition, this information is often difficult to use outside its original context. Cross-platform transferability - the ability to use the same data in different systems - is often not possible. The landscape of information processing is fragmented because of historical evolution and due to contradictory commercial interests. There are also some fundamental limitations. The data may be highly structured and intended as input for special applications: for example, three-dimensional CAD files and simulation models of product behavior are meaningful only when interpreted. CAD files must be rendered in two dimensions, and behavioral models simulated according to initial parameters. Emerging Web technology has improved this situation, as document description languages such as HTML and XML, the Java programming language, and common picture formats offer de-facto standards for rendering data into human-readable form, whenever it is possible and necessary.

We will now take a different viewpoint. Instead of looking at technical envelopes for information, we review the product design process and describe the information in general terms. The purpose is to illustrate the resources for sharing information among teams and interest groups, and to be used as material for culture and knowledge creation.

☐ Design communication:
  Especially in the initial design phase, the design team creates and consolidates a shared view of the design task. The communication takes place within design teams, but also among other stakeholders such as customers, sales and marketing, and production. It is typical that communication consists of drawings, drafts, clay models, discussions, and so on, which are difficult to document electronically. On the other hand, in this phase it is both necessary and useful to process information about pervious designs, as paragons and concrete examples, to be reused with modifications.
  There is often no strong natural computer support for this phase, although e-mail and message-based collaborative environments can be used. In addition, there is usually no established location or context to store the early communication information.
  An unfortunate practice is keeping design communication in personal archives. This data is often discarded after the project has been completed.

☐ Project control:
  Project control information is collected in standard form, either as pre-defined and controlled documents, or as data files generated by project control software. This information is stored at least during the project. This data type is important for supporting and documenting decisions and it also reflects design discourse.

☐ Design result files:
  These files are intermediate and final data products, which describe the designed artifacts, and provide support and evidence of their performance. Result files describe the design objectively, and are used in subsequent phases to create data for production, customer support and maintenance. In software design, the files are close to the final

product: they are compiled to binary form, and copies of these files are used as components of the final product. Design result files are created under controlled conditions. They are also archived for reference and product updates as well as new versions.

☐ Product data:
Product data files are derived from design files and from previous product data files. They are usually kept in on-line databases, and stored in electronic archives for reference. Changes made in product data files are strictly controlled. Usually, there is a formal change request process, and changes are authorized and reviewed in specific change control boards.

Stores for knowledge

We have pointed out that knowledge is personal and social, rather than documented information. However, it is a common opinion, that it would be useful to support knowledge creation by systematically collecting the type of information which is actively used in the knowledge creation process. Collecting such data is especially important because from the learning viewpoint, the most important information is created and processed during the early phases in design, a large amount of this information is not in electronic form, and it is usually discarded after the process. Creating a knowledge support database is a challenging task, because the information is in a varied and nonstandard form. It is also difficult to know what the viewpoint and purpose are, for which such data might be later recalled.

There are many difficult issues with knowledge support databases. It is clear that they contain material which is unreliable and difficult to interpret outside its context. A straightforward approach is to establish a systematic and separate knowledge recording practice. However, the motivation to operate such a system parallel to already demanding product creating activities is questionable. It is also difficult to separate and classify information for a possible and undefined future use.

A contrary approach is to utilize the information which has already been collected. The collection process should be made transparent. Design information which is already in electronic form should be tagged and archived. Content-based search engines are an additional technical option to make information retrieval both flexible and more comprehensive. Finally, the early design phases should be supported by information technology, through provision of electronic documents and data intensive operating environments and platforms.

Design machine dashboard

Producing useful things with industrial methods is a dominant economical activity in modern societies. Industry has achieved its leading role through standardization and mechanization of manufacturing processes. Moreover, the manufacturing technology is provided by specialized industrial companies. At the same time, with new technology-intensive products, design has become a time consuming and critical issue requiring skilled professionals. Product design cost has become the primary expense element. This is especially evident in software products, as there is practically no manufacturing cost, and all remaining costs are due to distribution and marketing.

While the industry has mechanized and standardized product manufacturing, it is only natural that there are serious attempts to control and mechanize the product design process. Should not product design also work smoothly and with predictable results like a well-oiled machine? The only problem here is that product design is creative work and the production units are human beings. After all, design is not a control issue, it is a management issue. More precisely, it is a management and control issue, in which people are guided through objectives and available resources, and the progress of their work is monitored.

Many original design studies and textbooks have been made within the traditional machine industry. A German-based systematic industrial approach is presented in "Konstruktionslehre" by Pahl and Beitz [21]. Ferguson describes the evolution of design model catalogues since the Renaissance [8]. An approach towards formal design theory is presented by Nam Suh [29]. Regarding a product-focused approach, one of the most respected references is the excellent textbook of Ulrich and Eppinger [30]. Systems theories approach the problem from the perspective of artifacts. A good introduction is Derek Hitchin's book on application of systems theory in engineering [11], while Peter Checkland approaches the problem from a human viewpoint: how is it possible to understand and analyze complex systems [5]. In the software domain, the initial effort has been in making programs more comprehensible, starting from structured programming principles. Brooks' distinguished "The Mythical Man Month" [3] reflects the bitter experiences from the first large software projects. In recent years, visions of software engineering have integrated with more general engineering models. Software engineering research has pioneered in the application of process management methods in engineering. We also refer to some formal model and standards.

Solving the design problem

The art and skill of designing has fascinated philosophers and scientists. Designing has been investigated for decades, and not without results. Also in industrial settings, companies have developed their design methods, especially through practical experimenting. If we make a very crude division, we can separate two elements of product design: there is the creative element, which produces novel things, and there is the engineering element, which arranges the conditions and practical procedures to achieve the results. Although we want to point out that from an individual designer's viewpoint these two elements are inseparable, we feel it practical for our discussion to make this distinction. We have already addressed the creativity element. Now we will look at the practical arrangements and conditions needed to make product design a successfully organized and directed activity.

In our discussion, we repeatedly ask: "what do designers and engineers do?" Here, we consider one very concrete answer: they make models. The output of their work is a model of the product, created according to some viewpoint. A technical model is a description of the structure of the product: what kind of components the product is made of, how they are arranged and interconnected. A software designer describes how processor instructions are arranged and controlled, and this description is called a program. An industrial designer makes a model of the physical form and appearance of the product.

Models are used for communication within teams, and between different interest groups. For example, a model is used by a prototype workshop to build a prototype, or by manufacturing department to program production machines. The behavioral model or the functional model of the product do not describe the structure of the product, but are necessary for people who define the structure.

Design elements: function and form

The fundamental invention in design theory was the separation of function and form. The function is some abstract utility which the product shall perform. Thus, the task of the designer is formulated as a problem solving task: how to implement the function, using specifically shaped material objects and energy. Design theorists approach the solution through a systematic analytical method, which is a standard practice in sciences. The utility functions are decomposed into sub-functions and classified. This decomposition is repeated, until the design problem has been reduced to a collection of primitive functions. Now the theory assumes, that for each primitive function there are some implementation alternatives. For example, to fix two material pieces together one can use screws or rivets, and the choice can be based on the need to unfix the parts later. In principle, the designer could use catalogues of model solutions, and construct the design as a selection of alternatives. This systematic design method has also been included in the German industrial norm, VDI 2221 [31].

It is difficult to find the roots of this approach, but we do know that Renaissance engineers made sketches of elementary designs. Later, in the 17th and 18th centuries, large catalogues of model engineering solutions, "theatres of machines" were collected, published, and distributed in printed form and displayed in exhibitions. Such catalogues played an important role in disseminating new technology. The strength of this idea is obvious: creating fundamental design solutions is not a trivial task, and engineers prefer to use standard models or factory-made components instead of developing them - unless there is a good reason to do so. In a developed technical society, there are commercial companies who provide mass produced technical components for mechanical, electrical, electronics, pneumatic and hydraulic designs. In software engineering, products can contain a considerable amount of ready-made commercial modules. The software components market is less developed than other technical sectors - perhaps because there is no separate manufacturing phase, and maybe also because programmers like to begin work by creating the elementary components, to become familiar with the environment. Anyway, component markets are a significant element of a technical infrastructure.

Do engineers really apply this systematic, top-down design method? The answer is yes and no. Product development is a complicated process, which has an evolutionary and iterative character. According to the evolution analogy, product design progresses through gradual modifications of existing forms. We can also systematize modifications. We can use scaling, by increasing and decreasing some elements of the design. We can extrapolate design solutions beyond their nominal boundaries. We can transfer technical solutions to other kinds of designs, and we can integrate designs by combining functions, or separate them into smaller and more numerous units. Although there are few practical systematized methods, engineers do these modifications during the design process, as they try to analyze and improve their solutions.

The whole idea of an analytical engineering process can be criticized. It is an interesting philosophical question whether there really are abstract product utility functions. Could it be that technical opportunities create expectations and product ideas, and inspire new designs. Large and unique design projects are rarely executed. This can occur, for example, in the aerospace industry. Even in these cases, the designers are already aware of the undertaking, and a systematic method is needed to organize and rationalize the enormous engineering effort.

We feel that the systematic design model is not very useful as a template for new designs, but it is useful for analyzing existing designs and previous design phases. This analysis work can then be applied to improve the design. A typical analysis approach is to see how elementary product functions are allocated to product components. In a coupled design, physical elements perform several functions, and in de-coupled designs, each component performs a dedicated function [29, 30]. However, unlike proposed, it is generally not sensible to give merits to designs according their degree of coupling. Design merit depends on many other factors such as the needs of mass production, flexibility, reusing designs, and assembly costs and service options.

Analysis is important in the early product design phases, especially if we already know the overall design solution, and the functionality and technical performance have been demonstrated. Product performance may be demonstrated through earlier designs or laboratory prototypes, and sometimes also by computer simulation. Directing the analysis depends on our objectives. We discuss three different viewpoints: optimizing a single design, optimizing a product line and exploring user acceptability. Although we present the viewpoints separately, in practical design analysis, it is necessary to balance different viewpoints.

Optimizing a single design

As we described above, the systematic design process starts with clarifying a set of utility functions for the product: this is usually called requirements definition. Some of these requirements are expressed as functions or transformations that the system is to perform, while other requirements set limits and conditions for the design. The fulcrum of a systematic design process is then to convert the function structure into a structure of interconnected technological modules. In real situations, there are a number of possible implementation configurations, and the choice depends on external factors: usually there is a trade-off between product cost, and product usability and performance. Different product alternatives can be compared by scoring, using some criteria to define scores for utility functions and cost factors.

A practical method to illustrate the design problem is employing tables and matrices. The quality function deployment method (QFD) utilizes a specifically shaped matrix, where product functions are rows and implementation components are columns. Matrix representation helps to detect relationships between requirements and implementation elements. One objective is to determine, which feature is the cost driver. Many practical designs have a cost driver. For example, with a battery operated device, operating time is often a cost driver and a trade-off with product weight.

Optimizing product lines and platforms

Only in rare cases, when a product is very simple, or when it is extremely complicated, it is designed as a unique product. With a simple product design, cost is negligible, and with a complicated product, design and product cost is so high that no extra cost can be tolerated. In most cases, an industrial product is part of a product program or product family. The goal of product line optimization is to share design costs among several product models. A product program is a planned sequence of product releases, so that new, improved products can be launched, as required to fulfill market needs and to respond to competition. A product family is a set of simultaneous models with different features: to respond to the needs of different user segments, and to give consumers alternatives to choose from. Often, a product program includes parallel product families.

Product line thinking is based on modularity. Different models can share modules, and often the modules also have different life spans. Product modularity can be made visible to users, as with computers and instrumentation products. Modularity can also be hidden, and be only visible to product engineers. Strictly speaking, modularity is an inherent feature of technology, as practically all complicated products are modular, containing common, third party components.

A product platform is a related but wider concept. A platform may contain not only modules of current products, but also modules of future products, generic technologies, and tools and instruments. Platform thinking looks into the future and is built for continuity. Investments on the product platform have a longer time span than investments on an individual product. However, in practice, the distinction between platform and product components may be ambiguous. Often, product platforms emerge naturally, as a result of a series of individual product projects, and platform management as a distinct activity is initiated later.

Controlling and optimizing product lines is a more demanding task than optimizing a single product. On the other hand, it reduces business risk, as an unsuccessful product model can be rapidly replaced with a hopefully luckier model. It is a trade-off by offering external plurality, while internally companies try to control and reduce the amount of self designed as well as third party components.

Analyzing product concepts: the user's viewpoint

Analyzing the design economy is one reason for balancing product features with implementation features. The other important analysis objective is to explore the product concept. This analysis uses a similar approach, also based on the theoretical design model. A product concept is a certain combination of product features. Here the focus is on the needs and expectations of the user. While we can apply the described analysis techniques to find out the cost impact of each potential product concept, it is also necessary to be able to create illustrative models of the future product.

Concept exploration is a dialogue between product engineers, users and business specialists. In this social play, product engineers have an advantage, as they are more capable of interpreting drawings and drafts. The engineers may also be biased towards technical excellence and elegance. Industrial designers have important roles in this process, as they can act as mediators between technical highlights and application highlights. The ultimate success factor is user's acceptance.

The design concept should already please potential customers. It is also necessary to ensure, that the product is satisfactory when it is used in a realistic environment and employing its full functionality. We can see that the modern product design process tries to combine the two extreme points of the product creation process: the early definition of product concept, and the traditionally late validation of the final product. The ultimate goal is to validate the final product before it is designed!

Illustrative, faithful and early product representation is the key element in this process. Product simulation in different forms has become an important design support technique. Traditional mechanical mock-ups are being replaced by computer simulation or through the application of physical models with simulated functionality. We have been demonstrating the importance of product success, and this success is created by designing acceptable and desirable products.

Systems approach: world as a system

In design and engineering, systems theory approach aims to understand, analyze and explain technical objects. A system is seen as a collection of entities, which interact with each other, and with the environment. There are natural systems and artificial systems. The critical aspect is to recognize system boundaries. Actually, the concept of boundary is more or less artificial, and depends on the viewpoint. There may be natural boundaries such as the skin of an animal, which separates the animal from its environment. Often, there are no natural boundaries, for example, with organizational and social systems. With product engineering, it is fruitful to analyze the product boundary: what is the environment that is interesting with regard to the product, and what kind of interactions are there. When analyzing a product, it is useful to distinguish three different systems: the technical system (the product), the physical product environment and the human activity environment. An advanced analysis question is to consider the service which the product provides as a system. Where are its boundaries and what interactions exist?

Systems thinking: understanding systems

Systems thinking is a method for analyzing and modeling systems. It is especially valuable with large and complicated systems, for example, technical infrastructures. There is no limit, how complicated such an analysis can be, as the real world contains an endless amount of details and features. A rational analysis is only possible through a systematic simplification procedure, in which the analyzer deliberately excludes elements of the target object from consideration. By repeating such exclusions, the analyst finally can construct a model, which is not an accurate image of its target object, but is reasonably small to be understood and discussed by human beings.

Our purpose is not to be pessimistic about system models. Rather we want to point out that any model is made according to some viewpoint and purpose, and is a coarse simplification. So we should not take a given model as granted, but to apply a dialogue and social discourse, until we feel that we understand its scope and limitations, and possibly make some updates in the process.

Systems engineering: creating systems

We describe systems engineering as a rational and holistic model to create a design, so that all aspects of the design are taken into account: (1.) all components of the artifact which have to be designed, (2.) the environment, where the future artifact is to be used and utilized through its life cycle; and (3.) organization of the human activities which create the design. Thus, it is actually a full model for designing.

The systems engineering model is derived from the general design theory we discussed above. It is a sequence of constructive activities, which refine and transfer the requirements for a product into a description of the product structure. It also includes a verification track, which assures that the design is correctly made in the technical sense, and that it fulfils the requirements.

The model also considers the product as a system: it considers the product as a collection of subsystems, defined according to their functions. The product is also decomposed according to technical discipline: for example, divided into mechanical, electronic, software, thermal, electromagnetic, industrial design and usability domains.

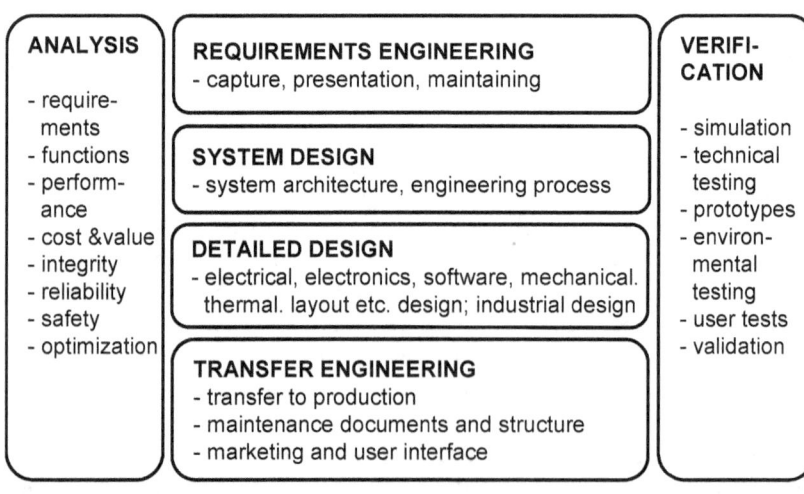

Figure 7. Elements of the systems engineering process-

One representation of a general systems engineering model is illustrated in figure 7. In the early phases of the design effort, the requirements for the product are explored, defined and compiled into a suitable form to be used as a mission for the subsequent engineering phases. System design defines the overall structure, the architecture of the product, both in terms of product sub-functions and different engineering disciplines. Within each technical domain, the detailed structure is then defined. Systems engineering is finalized by the transfer engineering phase: the necessary information is produced to utilize the design - information for production, maintenance, training and customers.

There are two specific techniques to address the quality of the created models. Analysis applies mathematics and technical theories to make conclusions of the design, when it is still in the conceptual or abstract phase. Verification techniques are applied to components and modules when they are given a detailed structure. A typical verification technique is testing.

Although the layout in figure 7 seem to suggest a certain direction of progress, we stress that the sequence and scheduling of the activities is flexible, and depends on the actual situation and nature of the product. Especially important is that three activity classes are implemented throughout the engineering life cycle.

1. In all phases, the progress and intermediate results are compared against the requirements
2. The analysis activity is applied whenever possible, both during the determination and decomposition of requirements, as well as during the constructive design phases
3. The verification activity is applied repeatedly during the constructive design phases.

It should be understood, that a product is seldom designed as a single effort. Rather, a typical complex product is a collection of modules, subsystems and platform elements on different levels of maturity, and each of those elements is created more or less separately. Usually the creation of a final product model an integration and design update process. However, each design efforts involves selected elements of the generic systems engineering process.

We will next describe how these elements can be mobilized in a manageable social activity. We will need yet another method: process management.

Process approach: the design machine

When the elements of designing are organized into a coordinated and controlled effort, we can apply another concept: process management. The roots of process management have a long history. The concept has been borrowed from manufacturing industry. Systematic ways for organizing work can be found through the history of large-scale manufacturing. However, perhaps it was the pioneers of quality engineering in the 1950s, such as Joseph Juran in the USA and Kaoru Ishikawa in Japan, who applied the power of analysis to address the performance of manufacturing processes, and arranged their techniques into organized quality management practices.

The advantage of process management is that it addresses both performance and content of activities. Processes describe the actual activities performed within the organization. They have the capability to bypass functional and hierarchical - more or less artificial - superstructures, and allow focusing on the essentials.

The traditional design process adopted during the first half of the 20th century is a linear and progressive sequence, from the definition and refinement of the requirements to construction and testing a prototype. NASA adopted this model for aerospace projects and introduced an important improvement: the phased project planning method, PPP. The design process was decomposed into sequential phases, and after each phase there was a review. Only after a successful review and resolution of review issues was proceeding permitted to the next phase. The important process elements, the activity phases and the review, are still the basic elements of a controllable design process.

This linear design sequence, which is generally also known as "the waterfall model" is very good for large projects, which are to produce a complicated, unique product. Often, the product is not satisfactory after the first design run. In reality, the process has to be repeated, and each time the result improves. This arrangement is called the spiral model. Even the spiral model is unsatisfactory in most practical cases. In the iterative model, the product is designed through a series of small design steps and modifications. This is a feasible model especially for software, where building non-physical prototypes for testing is a fast and automated procedure. Many design projects are actually improvement projects, where some modules of the product are redesigned. As product line and product family thinking is advancing, product development is actually performed as many parallel design projects, which are more or less coordinated.

In modern product development, managers must control a group of design processes. When each individual project is planned, engineers have to decide, which elements of the systems engineering process are included, and how to build a review and control structure to manage the efforts.

Control room: managing and monitoring design

We begin with a birds eye view: analogically with the practice of industrial production, industrial product development activities can be seen as a layout of design units. There are the issues of sequencing activities, storing intermediate products, raw materials and resources, external subcontractors, and queues because of limited capacity of critical production units. A considerable difference is that design is creative and mental work. It cannot be observed directly, but must be made visible through intermediate results and review activities.

According to industrial tradition, a key element in technical progress is standardizing design methods and practices. Shared understanding is made easier through defining general and widely known models. In the preceding paragraphs, we have described these models. The rest of design instrumentation is accomplished through planning and documentation techniques. Engineering models define documents and document handling procedures, which are to be used to communicate design content and progress.

Project management appears to be one of the most general and uniform industrial processes. It was originally developed for large construction projects, to control and schedule multiple activities and their mutual dependencies. However, project management appeared to be useful to control any bounded activity, especially if the task is non-trivial, risky and unpredictable. This is why product design is usually performed within the project envelope. A product development effort is planned as a project - or often an ensemble of projects.

In a product development project, planning is necessary to consider what kind of engineering process should be applied and how to implement it. More precisely, it is decided, what elements of the engineering model are included, and how the elements are sequenced and scheduled. This implementation is then compiled into a project plan. The project plan usually defines the documentation structure: documents describing the design, and control documents. Management activities are also needed. We will now take a closer look at setting up the overall engineering project instrumentation:

- Project plan:
  The plan is the primary document about the effort to be performed. It is a road map, which has to be followed. Because the road is insecure, the relevance of the project plan must be reevaluated periodically during the project. It is often necessary to update the plan.
- Project leader:
  It has appeared practical to nominate one person within the project to perform day-by-day management activities.
- Control organization:
  There are many possible control arrangements depending on project size and criticality. Control may be accomplished through a project supervisor, a dedicated control board or a shared board.
- Project budget, schedule and resource plan:
  These elements are used to fit the project on the factory floor together with other projects. They are part of a project plan, and also under continuous control.
- Project control documents:
  The most important documents are progress reports, which contain a digest of control data: use of resources and progress of work. It is important to compare resource use with the work done; without this comparison resource use reports are meaningless. One important indicator is the estimation of remaining work. If the sum of work done and the work to be done is increasing, the project is in jeopardy. Control documents may also include milestone records such as review and test reports.
- Content documents:
  These documents contain coded results of design activities. They are necessary for communication within the project, and between the project and other interest groups. As the most important documents are produced according to plan, they also serve as milestone indicators.
- Reviews:
  Reviews are an important and efficient project control technique. Reviews may be planned beforehand. They are usually synchronized according to important internal node points: for example, a review of drawings is necessary before they are sent to the prototype workshop. Some reviews are internal to projects, while external stakeholders and experts may participate in the most important reviews.

Bridge: managing the product and product portfolio

In the paragraphs above we have illustrated the management of the design machinery. We referred to the control room analogy: the task of the control room is to assure that the design machinery is running smoothly, and to act and remedy possible disturbances. However, the technical and process vision is a necessary, but not sufficient viewpoint for product development. Product development business operates in a changing world, and activities which are currently in progress may have been initiated years before. Thus, it is necessary to perform higher level control and management activities. We will suggest another, supplementary analogy: the bridge of a ship.

The duty of the bridge is to be aware of what is taking place on board, but its most important task is to look around: what is happening in the outside world. Managing a product-based business means continuous navigation: looking for changes in the environment and updating current plans. The decisions on the bridge may alter or prioritize current projects, key resources, update platforms and product programs, and define urgent new projects. As we have highlighted the importance of product stakeholders, in the company context, it also means that the stakeholders are involved with the bridge operations.

A popular model for enterprise management is the performance pyramid model, which has a large number of variations. One common and simplified view is presented in figure 8. Usually, at the top there is the strategy layer, which is responsible for strategic planning, visioning and setting objectives. The strategy is then refined into plans and management activities. On the following levels are the processes which create the results of the company, and the resources which empower the processes. This popular picture provides a simple scheme for understanding the basic corporate structure. Regarding product-based business, the essential processes are those for product creation, and the activities which direct the product creation process.

We want to complement the picture with external stakeholder groups: shareholders, employees, resource networks and customers. Especially, we want to highlight the carriers of the stakeholder relationship. Regarding shareholders, the relationship is financial: the profit and added company value, which are created through business operations. Here, the time span is critical. The product-based business is dynamic and requires fast reacting, but under the restless surface are the long waves of technological and infrastructure evolution. Sustained leadership and profitability require long-term planning, and carefully selected strategies.

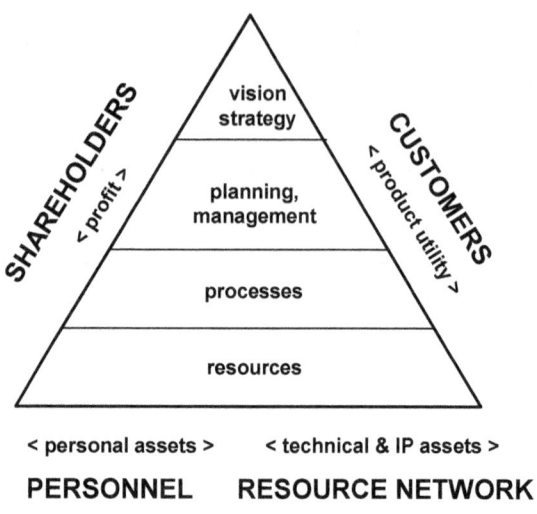

Figure 8. A management model of an industrial company with functions, resources and stakeholders.

Employees, for example capable product engineers plan, create and distribute the products. Although it is generally accepted that technology development is evolutionary and self-correcting, the performance of product designers has a significant impact on the efficiency of the product creation process. Product developers are especially motivated by design challenges and opportunities to learn and develop their professional skills.

Resource networks are necessary to empower the technological processes. According to the contemporary open innovation paradigm, external resources are needed to supplement product and technology creation (Chesbrough [6]). Especially technology-intensive products are far too sophisticated for any single company to master. Technologies are acquired, exchanged, licensed and co-developed in resource networks. Those networks involve subcontractors, partnering companies, commercial technology brokering, and research organizations. Even customers and consumers may be valuable members in resource networks, because they posses important application information and knowledge of user value processes.

Customers are among the most important stakeholders. Many companies employ special customer satisfaction and customer relationship management activities. The rudimentary fact remains that customers seek industrial products as instruments to arrange and manage their everyday lives, in work and leisure. The main carrier of the stakeholder relationship is the product.

Standard methods and best practices: where to find them

Product design methods and procedures are proprietary and company confidential, at least on the detailed level. On the other hand, many practices are common and quite uniform. A kind of de facto standardization arises, naturally and culturally, as companies learn from each other, and as employees migrate between companies. In the academic world, management and engineering research aims to find common behavioral patterns, as a starting point for analysis. Governments, professional societies and industrial clusters often try to publish and promote certain practices and models, to improve efficiency and to make co-operation easier. Standards are important information sources and useful references: if there are efficient and mature methods, there probably are also corresponding standards.

Standards are issued by national authorities, or by international and public standardization bodies. They may be also issued by voluntary private bodies such as industrial associations. A strong company may wish to create a de facto standard alone, to achieve a firm position on markets. Finally companies may issue internal standards to be applied in internal operations. Standards are usually compiled to create compatibility: if products and operation procedures have common features, co-operation between companies is easier. For example, a commonly agreed product infrastructure defines a market area in which compatible products can be sold and used. An infrastructure standard such as the GSM mobile telephone standard is a good example of successful infrastructure standardization. There are also mandatory legal regulations, which can be thought of as standards.

There are also small-scale standards. When product components are standardized, these components can be mass produced and sold for an affordable price. Such component standards are another form of technical infrastructure. For example, there are standards for battery sizes and voltages. Because standardization enhances competition, some companies adopt a policy of not adhering to standards to avoid competition: customer cannot buy a compatible product from another vendor.

Another reason for standardization is to propagate some practice which is considered to be useful. Quality standards are one example, and there are process standards. Although the main purpose of process and quality standards is to improve operational efficiency and to reduce waste, they also promote co-operation, as operations become more similar and compatible.

There are different reasons why companies act upon a standard: they may be obliged to, or they may be interested in adopting a standard, if they believe that a large number of other companies are also doing the same. Alternatively, they may simply want to adopt a practice and use a standard as a trusted reference. What we are most interested in is to promote a commonly agreed upon good way of operating.

When standards are used as references and models for working, one should consider how faithfully the practices should be implemented. Because standards are for general use, they can be much more complicated than is necessary from a company's viewpoint.

"Best practices" are like standards, common and preferred procedures of good conduct. Professional and industrial societies have made efforts to identify and promote best practices, to improve performance of their branch of activity. However, there are some dangers. As company practices reflect the local culture and conditions, they are also dependent on local knowledge. We have explored the nature of knowledge and explained why knowledge transfer is difficult. Thus, the direct transfer of best practices may contain a risk of failure.

We will not present a comprehensive review of standards, as the topic is too wide and there is the problem of selecting the standards are worth mentioning. Rather, we will briefly discuss some product development related activity domains, where method and procedure standards have emerged. We also will not discuss technology standards, but only general, technology independent ones.

□ Product creation:
  There are few general guidelines for product creation and design. Perhaps one of the most known methods is published by the Association of Engineers (VDI), which is intended for "traditional" mechanical products [31]. Product creation is a rather specific issue, which depends on technology and business features. In many companies, product creation is a highly confidential issue. However, there are systems engineering standards, which describe product creation from a more technical viewpoint. In addition, some quality standards describe requirements for product creation procedures.

□ Project management:
  Project management has become a mature and universal activity. There are standards published by industrial associations and by standardization bodies. Many large companies and organizations have also compiled internal project management guides and handbooks. Although a number of standards and guides exist, they are surprisingly uniform in content.

□ Design and engineering:
  Standards for design and engineering have originally been created for machine design. Recently, there has been significant development of software engineering standards. Systems engineering models describe

a general purpose technology development engineering cycle. Complementary standards are directed toward specific areas, especially for software engineering. Many design standards have originally emerged in the military and aerospace sector, for large, unique design efforts. More iterative and flexible models have been created for software. There has also been interesting evolution in software design standards: in addition to the traditional reference standards, there is an increasing body of standards, which are aimed at process assessment and process improvement.

☐ General modeling:
Modeling standards are defined to support definition and description of abstract product features. We provide some examples of the areas where such detailed methods have been used. The definition of software algorithms and protocols has traditionally used schematic and formal techniques such as flow charts and state diagrams. The development has led, for example, to the widely known protocol definition language, SDL, and the universal modeling language, UML. The IDEF (Integrated Definition language) models are a group of modeling methods that can be used to describe various operations and processes within companies, as well as for modeling different product aspects. It was originally created by the United States Air Force for manufacturing activities. Each of the IDEF methods are designed to capture a particular type of information. Programming languages and document description languages are in intensive use. They are actually abstract product modeling standards, very formal, and often technology and vendor specific. Their specific feature is that they are computer-readable, so their use is "mandatory" and they have to be implemented accurately.

☐ Quality standards:
Quality improvement methods and standards have originally emerged from the manufacturing industry. However, they have found wide use in all types of organizations, and are applied in product development with increasing frequency. Actually, the widely used ISO 9001 reference standard defines requirements for the product creation process. There are also quality standards for assessment and improvement of quality (so-called quality award approach). These standards do not contain exact requirements for product development processes, but leave organizations an opportunity to choose the actual methods and procedures. We can also consider process improvement standards as a class of quality standards.

☐ Product standards:
Product standards define requirements for products. They are needed for product compatibility with user systems and other products. An important type of product standard are infrastructure standards, for

example, for transferring data and applications. Good examples are standards for electrical power, mobile phones and Internet protocols. There are both product specific and general standards. There are also regulations for general safety and protection, regarding property, human life, technical systems and the environment.

Matching products with markets

In this chapter, we describe how product design relates to the other business activities of an industrial company. We emphasize technology and knowledge, product planning and marketing.

Several studies of the significance of product development for companies are reported by Walsh et al. [33]. The significance of product innovations, customers and changes in the operation environment are described in the classic work by Joseph Schumpeter [25]. Ulrich and Eppinger [30] provide a versatile presentation of product design, including the modularity concept and prototyping. We appreciate the concept of product simulation thorough models and prototypes as important elements in product creation [24]. The allocation of product functions and design efficiency are discussed by Suh [29]. Human decision making capability is considered in terms of the decision making theories of Herbert A. Simon [26]. Bruno Latour's "Aramis" illustrates the relationship between product innovations, infrastructures and politics [14].

Technology base of product design

Technology is the critical resource in product industries. Technology is needed to maintain and host existing products, and to develop new products. Companies have alternatives when acquiring new technology. It is possible to develop the technology with owned resources, or it can be acquired from existing sources. External sourcing can include buying a license, or buying a company or part of a company that owns the technology, or through a cooperation or partnership agreement. The license for external sourcing can be a transfer of ownership or a license to use the technology. Whatever the acquisition method, the acquirer needs some initial skills and knowledge of the technology.

What do we mean by technology? It can be a specific product or a sub-domain of a product or product family, for example, speech recognition technology for a voice command terminal. It can also deal with manufacturing, for example, assembly and processing machinery. Whatever the characteristics and boundaries of the technology, it usually has the following components:

☐ Intellectual property rights: patents, models and trademarks if granted; paternity rights, which protect the right of the creators to use and exploit a unique design

☐ Documentation: design and production documents as well as supporting documents such as service instructions, technical manuals, user's documents, and marketing and training material

☐ Physical prototypes: mock-ups, partial prototypes and fully operational prototypes

☐ Instruments needed to maintain the technology: tools, computer software and production equipment

☐ Knowledge about using, producing, maintaining and further developing the technology

The most natural way to acquire new technology is to develop the technology in-house. A generic product development process is also a comprehensive technology creation instrument. The difficult part in technology acquisition is gaining knowledge about the technology, and is the strongest point in favor of creating technology internally. The product engineering process first creates product definition documents, which are then transferred to other necessary documents and prototypes, and human knowledge is gained during the design and design transfer process. Although self development is the most efficient producer of knowledge, it is usually also the most expensive and time consuming alternative. Especially if the technology is new or immature, there may be enormous risks. Some innovations require years or decades to develop into working technology, or are impossible to utilize at all.

The alternative is to buy or license technology. This is faster and probably less expensive. However, there is a considerable risk that the adoption process fails because of a failure to create or transfer the necessary knowledge. This phenomenon has been best demonstrated through unsuccessful attempts to transfer technology between industrialized and developing countries. Without its cultural background, technology will loose its functionality. The same may occur within a country, between different industrial cultures. Knowledge and culture are not attached to documents, but to people.

If technology is well established and in common use, it can be taken into use and utilized relatively easily: general technical education and experience of common industrial culture are sufficient. Although some time and work is necessary to learn the specific details and properties, technology adoption is not impossible. However, special care must be taken if the technology is new, or if the cultural background of the technology source and recipient are very different. There are ways to facilitate the knowledge acquisition part of technology transfer. A straightforward method is to buy technology together with personnel, for example, by buying a company or part of one. Even in this case, there is a risk that key persons leave their positions, or that the transition to a new organization culture is not smooth. It is also possible to rent personnel for a limited time, to work together with the recipient's personnel until they have adopted the technology. Because the most practical method of gaining knowledge is hands-on work with the technology and prototypes, an attractive alternative is to set up a shared product development project, where persons from both companies participate.

Exploring product features and market response

It is clear that product developers should be able to match product features with customer needs. Even more important is that customers prefer the product to competitors' products. Industrial economics, management and innovation research have created and documented a variety of theories and techniques for analyzing markets and product palettes. However, it seems that a product-based business is a game where the main players are the company, the competitors and the consumers. As with other games, some players win and some loose, even when all the players know the rules.

In the last few decades, product development textbooks have emphasized the importance of listening to customers. However, the customer is not the only stakeholder outside of the core design team. In the mid 1980s, the "concurrent engineering" concept[17] introduced two important principles:

---

[17] In literature, concurrent engineering is sometimes presented with a narrow meaning: accelerating product development by performing tasks in parallel.

1. All product interest groups should participate in the product development process. These include the end users/customers.
2. The product development process must be transparent. That is, all product related information, including the discussions and contributions of product interest group members should be visible to all participants.

The drawback of the concurrent engineering concept is that it was proposed and evolved in the military and aerospace contracting community, and was targeted towards the development of complicated and large systems. The assumption was a unique product development process. Those projects had been conducted, for example, for NASA. Such heavy projects lasted for years, so that a thoroughly designed development process, with well planned analysis and verification phases, was necessary.

Surprisingly, it became apparent that a completely different product development process benefits from concurrent engineering principles: development of demanding consumer products. The need to reduce product development time and costs has forced new approaches. The leading idea is the transition from one large development process to a series of small, iterative work efforts, which can be studied, controlled and validated separately. There are many implementations for this development thinning approach. The platform method applies modularity: products are made up of modular components, and old and new components can be mixed in prototypes and new designs. Supplementary techniques include building prototypes with reduced functionality, applying non-representative implementation technology (rapid prototyping), and digitally simulating functional and physical properties (virtual prototyping). There is also the heterogeneous prototyping method, where real, reduced and simulated product modules are mixed in product prototypes.

Lightweight prototyping technology adds a new dimension to product technology: playing around with product prototypes. The prototype game can efficiently be played in product development teams. A product prototype can be made the focus of attention and communication, and an organizer of shared tasks. This is especially attractive with virtual prototyping technology, where the first prototypes can be created very early in the project, actually already during the research and concept definition phase. It can be also shared through electronic media, so that prototyping is no longer bound to location. Prototyping strongly supports cross-functional product development within companies. It also makes it easier for external parties such as subcontractors, technology partners and customers to join in. For example, the marketing department may want to create an early prototype, and use it in market studies.

There are higher business risks in developing new products. This is largely because there is no paragon for the product. Customers are not familiar with the product concept, and it is probable that the composition of the product concept or architecture is not correct. Prototyping is one way to proceed, but one should also remember that any product is also a prototype - a prototype for subsequent models and future success. It is the ultimate and most realistic prototype. A company entering new markets and new product technology should be prepared to learn from the experience and to introduce the next model evolution at a suitable moment. A deliberate and controlled method for involving customers in product validation is beta testing, employed especially in the software industry. A beta prototype is given to selected key customers, often free of charge, with the obligation to report errors and product performance.

Prototypes are not only useful for developing new products. They can be also applied to developing innovations. It takes time before an innovation is recognized and becomes a marketable product. A well known historical example was the development of the zip fastener. During some 60 years several tentative forms of the zipper were designed and experimented with in pioneering products, but the invention remained marginal. Only when a proper form was finally found, together with a right application area and economical mass production method, the zipper became a profitable product. Often in industrial history, analyzers claim that some product was introduced too early. However, the coin has a flip side. The early and unsuccessful product versions were necessary to make the innovation known and to collect consumer feedback. Correctly timing a product launch may include launching unprofitable pilot products to probe markets.

There is also the late entry strategy. Developing leading-edge high-technology products can be prohibitively expensive. Companies that are in the first line of technology often pay an extremely high price for developing breakthroughs in critical design and technology. Typically, they have to develop the missing technological and innovation infrastructure, which then becomes almost a free commodity for the followers. The late entry policy is definitely not risk-free either because a technology follower is always in a more difficult competitive position. The only benefits that the follower enjoys are savings in development costs. There is also the risk of loosing touch with the technology and entering the markets too late. Such risks may also be mitigated through prototyping techniques: to keep the product team in touch with product technology and to develop the features based on mature technologies, while simulating the immature ones.

Product strategies and product planning

The task of product strategy is to match resources and capabilities with market needs. Naturally, the development of a product strategy is market driven and based, for example, on customer segmentation and market research and analysis. Analyzing the market situation looks at external dynamics such as the life cycle and maturity of a product, overall sales potential, penetration and growth, product life, and the replacement of old products. Competition analysis tries to find basic competition strategies; the competitors and their capabilities. Channel analysis considers product distribution routes and the consuming logic of customers. All this is difficult and demanding. However, this is only one side of the coin: the world of abstract needs and abstract business games.

When we consider manufacturing and marketing technology intensive products, the product itself becomes important. Market research and customer segment analysis is worth doing only if we have a firm product concept. Is this possible on new technology markets? We have two provocative proposals, which we hope to illuminate with our product case examples. The proposals are:

1. There are no abstract consumer needs
2. We cannot plan optimal products, only products that are limited by our capabilities and restrictions.

We will take a closer look at the propositions, and consider their consequences.

"There are no abstract consumer needs." How can we listen to customers if they have nothing to say! Hold on, we did not say that consumers have no needs. We just want to remind, that products are the technology, which the consumer needs to organize his everyday life: for immediate and urgent commonplace activities and to make life a little more tolerable or even enjoyable. A consumer's need horizon is spanned by his imagination, and conception of his resources and possibilities. In other words, if you show the consumer what is possible, he may very well be interested.

Recent history is full of examples of how new previously unimaginable inventions are finally accepted into everyday life: the telephone, radio and television. Some modern innovations are equally shocking on closer inspection: not even science fiction writers or systematic technology forecasts of the Rand Corporation could predict, that consumers would want to buy computers into their homes only 25 years later. It seems that emerging technology creates new needs, and new products to fulfill the needs. Although this phenomenon is sometimes called "technology push," it should not be understood literally. The consumer cannot be pushed. Rather, the process of innovation is a discussion or social play. In a social discussion, new ideas are projected against the characteristics and opportunities of the real world. When some of those ideas, implemented through technology, make the world change, new opportunities emerge and new ideas are stimulated.

It is easy to see, that this dialogue is public, and that the parties which create public information are the key players in this process. Media, universities, research centers and educational institutes promote this process; as do companies, by distributing their products and associated technical documents, instruments and services to create new ways of utilizing technology and new needs. We want to point out, that it is not only a question of listening to the customer, but taking active part in the discussion between customers and other players.

"There is no optimal product." This claim, although it may sound acceptable in principle, requires further consideration. First, we consider the product as above, through our systemic viewpoint. A single product model has a limited life span: it wears out, and evolving technology makes the old models obsolete. It reflects technological possibilities, and together with consumer and market reaction it suggests characteristics for the next model. In a dynamic situation, the product also faces a risk of failing or at least being seriously challenged by competing products. The company should be able to guess the most suitable product configuration for the market. The company should also be prepared to develop and launch the next product models, and be fast enough react to consumer responses and competitors, and make the necessary changes and improvements. All product companies face the pressure of resource consuming product development. It is not only a question of money. It is also a schedule issue, and a question of knowledge and technology resources, product development efficiency, and manufacturability and production costs. Product development is a complicated issue, but the advantage of complicated issues is that they offer wonderful opportunities. A skilful player who is aware of his own strengths and weaknesses can find opportunities and create a successful product line. In real life, David has as hard time defeating Goliath, but in the product development business, this situation is common. Regarding the market and innovation setting we described, it can be understood that a failure or sluggishness to react to new market situations by altering practices is more probably a problem for large, established companies.

Is the market and competition setting we just described somehow different, if we consider new innovations and complicated high technology products? We claim that there are additional concerns. With new, evolving innovations, the product concept is also under change. Thus, the first products are often more like prototypes. They should none the less They should none the less be well-designed. A bad prototype may spoil the image of the company, and in the worst case hamper the evolution of the innovation. Another concern is that developing a new, complex product requires time. Even if the developer is familiar with the technology, the development process may require several years. On the other hand, the dynamics of the marketplace may require that the company has several models simultaneously on the markets, and new models have to be introduced every year.

Modularity - a way to optimization and mass customization

The normally adopted solution for managing product mix and technology leveling issues is product modularity. The theoretical base of modularity comes from the axiomatic design theory. The abstract design process decomposes the product function into sub-functions, and allocates an implementation module for each function. In integrated or "coupled" designs one module may implement a number of functions, while in modular designs there are more modules and less functions per module. The general rule in design is that integrated designs are more efficient in terms of material and energy use and more economical in mass production, but they are also more expensive to develop and difficult to modify. The evident lesson is that complicated products should be modular.

However, the modularity concept is much more, than just a way to optimize the design process for a certain amount of mass produced items. It has the power to satisfy consumers expectations. As consumers are individuals and they have different needs, they need to choice between product alternatives. Modularity allows product companies to offer a range of different product models, without the need to re-design for each model. And even more, even the same product model may be modified for individual needs - a process sometimes called product configuration. The following example illustrates different aspects of modularity.

A product may have a structural frame (where its modules are fixed) and a cover (to protect the internal parts from the environment, to protect the users and to provide a pleasing appearance). If the frame and cover are integrated, assembling the product becomes faster and its weight is reduced. However, an integrated cover with supports for fixing other modules may require a demanding three-dimensional design process, and the manufacturing start-up cost is high because an expensive casting mould has to be produced. An opposite example is that many cellular phone manufacturers provide designs where the user can alter the appearance of the device by changing the outer cover. Here, an extra module - the interchangeable cover - was introduced to fit the product to diverse consumer groups and to provide consumers with a new feature. The extra cover will surely introduce extra cost: new, demanding design and an extra part to manufacture and assemble. The cover also provides some tangible benefits: better protection and longer product life - something which the consumer surely both understands and appreciates. Our cover examples also illustrate that there is no simple truth.

Software intensive products have interesting modularity properties. Many intelligent products have a lot of functionality, and the software implementation is modular. However, it is possible to conceal this modularity from the user, through applying an integrated user interface. A personal computer is an example of a product, where a considerable part of the modularity is not concealed, and the consumer is usually left with a confusing and disturbing experience of its use. A cellular phone is an example of a software intensive product, where functional modularity is concealed from the user. For example, making a call requires only a few simple operations.

Modularity has several application forms. It allows defining product families - products which share common features. Making product variations and new models is also much easier. Products can be tailored for different user segments. Expensive parts can be shared among different models, and manufacturing lots can be made larger and development costs shared. Product design that is based on modularity is also called platform design. A product platform is a collection of designs and other technical items needed for product. A platform may support one or several product families or product lines. An extensive product platform is an important resource and technology depository. Platform life is much longer than product life. A product development company can also distinguish between platform projects and product projects. Planning platform projects is a strategic issue, as platform items should serve several products and future needs.

What has been said of product modules is also applicable to prototyping and virtual design. Prototypes can apply physical and simulated modules. Using prototypes composed of mixed technologies and mixed maturity modules is called heterogeneous prototyping. Prototype architecture is closely related with product architecture. To avoid unnecessary complications and artificial creation of prototyping interfaces, prototyping should be considered in the early phases of product architecture planning. Prototype modules should also be included as important elements in product platforms.

Product design champions

It seems to be a realistic approach to consider that industrial enterprises are guided through a sequence of more or less fortunate management decisions, and influenced by a series of internal and external incidents. Managers, engineers, investors and other players are doing their best to cope with the complex world. However, as Herbert A. Simon has pointed out, decisions are nevertheless based on bounded rationality: based on local minima, limited by the time to search for solutions, or simply restricted by the decision making mechanism. This is not a pessimistic view, if it is properly understood. It only means that decisions should be made on the assumption that they may be totally wrong, and a back-up strategy should be considered on some level.

Since the 19th century, engineers and product designers have lost their heroic position in society. Even today, there are product champions inside companies and behind the scenes. However, to the general public, the individuals who create the necessary technical product framework have become silent and unknown soldiers. Only occasionally, the industrial designer may be given a heroic role. Considering the large and complicated efforts for product development, this evolution is quite natural. Products are no longer created by individual artist-engineers, but by multi-disciplinary and cross-functional product teams.

Meanwhile, technical evolution and the growing demands for the product development workforce have changed the social status of engineers, from a major contributor and partner into a white collar worker. Today, engineers also know through experience that the entire product process chain from concept generation to production and marketing contributes to the innovation. Too often they have also seen how a well designed and technically perfect product misses public acceptance and large markets. The diminishing social status of product designers may be thought of as a source of disappointment and resignation. This is balanced by the engineers' tendency to be strongly content-oriented. Obviously, they can find satisfaction from the challenges of their technical tasks, and if they are lucky, they have the opportunity to celebrate the success of their product team.

Considering product based industry, we can be sure of one hard fact. If a company is going to succeed, consumers have to prefer their products over competitors' products. When new innovations are concerned, consumers have to be ready to change their behavior. Consumers are the everyday heroes, who organize their lives and daily activities in different ways with industrial products. As we have discussed, man is a technological animal, and along the lines of segregated social roles, technology is increasingly mediated by factory made products. Products may take different roles. They can stay in the background, providing necessary support for daily routines. These products are at their best when invisible, harmless and easily replaced. However, new, smart products may adopt a more active behavior. They are typically instrumental and communicate with their users via specially designed, mechanical and electronic user interfaces.

Part III
Transformation through products

From forest economy to high-tech economy

Finland used to be known, if it was known at all, as a distant country on the northern edge of Europe. A country of lakes and forests, sparsely populated with silent people, speaking a rare and difficult language and taking care of their own business. Although some artists and sportsmen are more or less famous and even might be recognized as Finns, nobody would have referred Finland as a country of industry and technology. But during the last decades of the 20th century something happened. Finnish high-tech companies entered global markets, and among them, the largely unknown Nokia suddenly came "from the cold" as one of the leading developers and producers of electronic consumer products. And this sudden appearance of Finnish industries was not due foreign investments or cheap mass production, as is the case with many Asian emerging industrial companies. It is rather the opposite: the Finnish companies conquered world markets with original, well engineered and carefully manufactured high technology products of excellent performance and quality. The 21st century Finland is still distant, cold and relatively un-known. But those who get in touch with it, discover a well working, efficient and technically advanced society which earns its living through applying and developing high technology.

We will use Finland as a case to illustrate features of modern, technology based industries. It appears that the Finnish industry could take advantage of external conditions, as well as of existing internal strengths and resources, and take a quantum leap. It discovered the secret formula of successful information age economy, which is based on industrial tradition, technical excellence and customer orientation. We will explore "case Finland": culture, mental atmosphere, resources, historical development and crucial actions which led to breakthroughs. Then we will present specific industrial cases: case Nokia, case Fiskars case Strömberg / ABB, and case Kone.

Finnish industry before independence

Until 1809 Finland was a Swedish province. After reformation, the church set up a successful education campaign. It was controlled by a much feared test: marriage was not allowed, unless the couple could read and write. Already more than 200 years ago most Finns could read and write in their own language. Another important development was establishing regular post service. The Finnish economy in the Swedish era was agricultural. There was some small scale industry: water powered sawmills, production of saltpeter for gun powder, and a few iron works - although known iron ores were too lean for large scale production. Main export products were fish and fur, tar, and saw products.

In 1809 Finland was joined to Russia and was soon given an autonomic political position. This period marked both early industrialization and cultural arousal. Russia wanted to weaken Finland's ties to Sweden, and many significant investment projects were initiated. Helsinki was made the capital, and prominent foreign architects were hired for planning and construction of cities, including Helsinki's impressive central quarters. In 1857 construction of railways was also started. Foreign industrialists were encouraged to establish industrial enterprises in Finland, and they built e.g. sawmills, pulp and paper factories and textile factories. National resources were mobilized around tar making and ship building. Finland became the major exporter of tar, and a fleet of hundreds of wooden ships sailed on all seas of the world. Tar export and shipping business marked the first steps of globalization, and they were surprisingly successful

The era was also culturally significant. Russian favored Finnish language against Swedish, which contributed to a nationalist- romantic movement. The cultural elite strived to create a truly Finnish culture, including own literature, own history, and fine arts based on national themes. For the first time, Finns started to think themselves as a nation and country. After the city of Turku burned down, the old university of the city was moved to Helsinki. From the mental point of view, it is interesting, that the education program of leading Finns was philological and political: science and technology had little role. It was considered necessary to create an educated class of Finns, who could serve as civil servants and politicians. Those who wanted to study engineering had to go abroad, e.g. to St. Petersburg or to Germany. In 1849, after a critical debate, the first polytechnic school was anyway established. The mental landscape of Finnish leaders remained pastoral, it was oriented towards the past agricultural society, which was idealized. This era initiated the dichotomy between the humanist-oriented cultural and political elite, and between a weak, disintegrated and non-uniform group of technically educated people. The cleft between the two cultures was born, and since those days it has remained as the mental status quo.

The19th century created a country with a democratic structure, literate population, and gradually, an education system based on equal opportunities. Industrialization was initiated, and although forest industry served as backbone, machine and electrical product companies started to appear.

Industrial development in independent Finland

The end of the Russian period in Finland was restless: repression, 1st World War, revolution in Russia, and in Finland, declaration of independency and civil war. Economical relations with Russia were cut, and the Finnish industry had to find new markets. Tar making and sail ships gradually became obsolete, but other industries recovered. Although forest industry dominated, new industries started to emerge. Machine industry was built mainly for domestic needs: equipment for agriculture, combustion engines for land and sea applications, train cars and locomotives, and machines for power plants. Already in the Russian era enthusiastic technicians and engineers established factories for electrical products. They were needed, when building of the national power distribution network was started. One notable Finnish industrialist of the time was Gottfried Strömberg, who started manufacturing of electric products already in 1889. And when radio broadcasting started in late 1920s, several radio factories appeared as pioneers of electronics industry.

In the second World War Finland suffered loss of human lives, rather than severe material destruction. In addition, in the years 1944-1952 Finland had to pay war indemnity to Soviet Union, in form of heavy industry products: machinery and ships. It was a significant challenge, because at the same time the shape of society jumped to urban and industrial direction: infrastructure had to be modernized, and new homes had to be built for solders returning from the front. War indemnity stressed the economy significantly, it required 5 to 15% of the state budget, and the level of investments decreased 15 to 50%. However, the obligations were fulfilled, and as a by-product, the capacity of the machine industry was much improved. It has been estimated, that the Finnish industry suffered to some extent, but at the same time the industry got a new, modern direction, from forest products to machine industry. A major new government owned machine manufacturing company Valmet (1944-1999) was established by combining state weapon factories. The company produced a large variety of products, from ships, tractors and locomotives to paper machines. Later it played a significant role as a the first major high technology exporting company: it started to modernize paper industry, and developed a revolutionary web forming system for paper machines.

Since 1952 war indemnities were transformed into a bilateral trade relationship: factories exported industrial goods, which the Soviet Union paid with their products - which was mostly fuel. This appeared beneficial for both parties[18]: Soviet Union received new technology and consumer goods, while Finland did not need to spend currency for fuel. And what was significant, Finnish companies had found access to large and stabile export markets. This arrangement allowed new investments in capacity and technology development. The bilateral trade arrangement remained and flourished until disintegration of the Soviet Union in the late 1980s.

The post war period marked the creation of industrialized Finland. A more active government policy was adopted: the industrial structure was strengthened through public investments. Government-owned companies were established on those sectors, which were considered vital for a modern, industrial country: fertilizer manufacturing, mining, production of copper and iron, pulp and paper factories, production and operation of telecommunication network, and energy production and distribution. Forest industry still had s strong position, and it was supported with export-friendly financial policies: the Finnish Mark was repeatedly devaluated to keep the export industry competitive. On education sector, the government policy was to support development of provincial cities. New universities were established outside the capital metropolis area. To supplement the R&D capability of industry, the Finnish government established[19] the Technical Research Centre of Finland (VTT); which later became the largest research institute in Scandinavia with nearly 4000 employees.

---

[18] At least officially the Soviet party was somewhat dissatisfied with the arrangement, and wanted more visibility to their high-tech products through Finland. Unfortunately the Soviet union did not have much to offer on this sector. To make the trade more balanced, the Finnish government acquired nuclear reactors, electric locomotives, missiles and MIG 21 fighter airplanes. Consumers in turn favored Soviet made cars because of their low price.

[19] VTT was originally established 1942, to develop substitutes for strategic materials and to monitor the quality of war materials industry.

Maturing for the giant leap

The war indemnity industry and the subsequent bilateral trade agreement with the Soviet Union were significant factors in transforming Finland into an industrialized country. It produced wood products, machinery and electrical products. The domestic consumer markets were small, although bilateral trade increased the market size. This was a working arrangement for a relatively closed post-war economy, but when the markets were gradually opened, it appeared, that the industry had hard time to compete with imported products, and even more difficult to go to global markets[20].

The industrial culture necessary for future high-technology products was created by the machine and electrical industry. However, another element was still needed: electronics and software. The roots of electronics industries goes to late 1920s, when radio broadcasting was started in Finland[21]. Several radio factories were established, and when television broadcasting was started in 1957, the factories also started manufacturing of television sets. Radio and television industry created the necessary knowledge on radio waves and high frequency electronics. From 1950s, radio telephones were introduced. Also the electronics department of Nokia started to manufacture radio telephones, for military, taxi cars and for other professional use. In the late 1970s, the Finnish industry had a lot of experience on radio technology. But at that time, it was generally assumed, that radio telephones are for small scale use by professionals, and real consumer markets are based on television sets. Nobody could anticipate the renaissance and boom of radio communication in the last decade of 20th century!

We now introduce the second element of the Finnish high technology industry: computers and software. Before the introduction of the PC, one main application of computers was industrial control. And in Finland, there was a serious need for computer control in the forest industry.

Even before the invention of the microprocessor, experimental computers were constructed in the universities, and new, moderately priced minicomputers were adopted for small scale office applications and in process control. In addition, he Finnish industry had created at least two

---

[20] There was at least one bright exception: Vaisala. Since 1944 this company has produced weather sonds, weather stations and industrial sensors, and more than 90% of production has been for export. The company operates on a very specific market sector, and since the beginning, it has enjoyed a reputation of making excellent products.

[21] Here we have to mention Eric Tigerstedt (1886-1925), "Finland's Edison", who had more than 400 patents. His most important invention was a sound system for movies, and a major improvement of the electronic tube, by making the electrodes co-axial.

original process control computer designs[22]. When the microprocessor was introduced, a large number of computer control applications were implemented, based on commercial microcomputer modules or on proprietary designs. A significant feature of those applications was the need for high reliability. Software had to be stabile, capable for uninterrupted operation, and also to cope with exceptional situations. Even fault tolerant designs were applied. The impact of the forest industry as the main application sector was, that when the first new high-technology information technology products were introduced, they were programmed by a generation of engineers with a tradition of high reliability and availability.

In addition to process control, the forest industry - and also the shipping industry - offered still one challenge: high power electric motors and their drive electronics. In industry, application of electric motors since 1900 was a success story. Especially alternate-current electric motors are compact, highly reliable, and require only little maintenance. However, controlling the rotation speed or power output of those motors is not easy. The emergence of power diodes, thyristors and high-current transistors in 1960s-1970s were the key technologies for powering motor drives. Strömberg Ltd. had wide experience on electric drives for paper and pulp mills, vehicles and ice breaker ships. It pioneered the use of inverters (devices, which change the frequency of alternating current) in the cars of the new metro of Helsinki, and soon inverters were offered to control all sizes of industrial alternate-current motors.

The telecommunications industry was fragmented into several private telephone companies, which operated local calls in most cities, and a state owned telecom company which served rural areas and long distance traffic. While the telephone represented a thoroughly mature technology, new technological opportunities could be seen in traffic automation and in building the trunk lines. The key technology was digitalization of trunk lines, a technology which was anticipated, when digital semiconductor electronics was introduced in 1960s. The Nokia company's telecommunication department started to develop equipment for trunk signal digitalization. When the microprocessor appeared in 1970s, a state owned telecom company Televa set up a project to develop a digital automatic telephone exchange. The exchange product DX 200 became later a flagship product of Nokia's network business. We now understand, that these developments were the first steps in building the new information society. They also created the necessary technology base for the new consumer products for that society.

---

[22] One design was the Selco 1000 mainframe computer for paper and energy industry, by Strömberg Ltd. The other design was the S-ODA minicomputer for sawmill industry, designed by Teuvo Kohonen, who later became one of the leading computer scientists. Due the rapid pace of computer development, these designs soon became obsolete, and only a small number of those early computers were actually built and installed.

We have explained, how the Finnish industry advanced during the post-war decades. It was developing skills and technology, and reached the level of industrialized countries. However, the industry was concerned of the considerable dependency on the trade with the Soviet Union, and was preparing for international competition. The problem was, that the Finnish technology industry was producing investment products, which required a lot of engineering work. The markets in turn were relatively small, and there were already strong foreign competitors. This was also true for process control industry, for example Honeywell and Siemens offered a line of advanced automation products.

The electronics industry went out for looking larger markets, and found the television industry. As a political action it was decided to invest public money on the national television picture tube factory, Valco, and the manufacturing process was then licensed from Hitachi. The factory was intended to serve as the backbone for the national television industry. It seemed to make sense, because the price of the picture tube dominated the component cost of a television set.

The Valco factory soon became the waterloo for the Finnish consumer electronics industry. It appeared, that there was already too much global picture tube manufacturing capacity. Transferring the production technology from Japan to Finland was not without difficulties, and the factory could not meet the required production efficiency. And as the final disaster, Nokia's takeover of European television factories some years later also failed: the factories were inefficient and out-dated. The Asian television factories exported excellent products with competitive price. It was nearly the end of Nokia: the former multi-industry giant had to sell other business areas and focus its activities on the only remaining branch: telecommunications[23]. Was this also the end of the Finnish consumer product industry? Not at all, and not even in the global scale. World is full of surprises.

We have presented the industrial branches, which were important for the future, high-technology society:

☐ The forest industry was an important client for evolving machine and automation industry.
☐ Industrial culture was established within metal and machine industry, dating back to 1649. The industries were expanded and modernized in the post-war period.

---

[23] It was not completely the end of the television industry, either. The last Finnish television factory, Finlux, operated until 2005. The company had a reputation of well-engineered products, but it failed because of technology. The company could not anticipate the breakthrough of flat screen televisions, and bankrupted with the storage full of picture tube televisions.

- ☐ The early radio and television industry created know-how on high frequency electronics.
- ☐ The automation industry and high power electronics industry established quality culture for electronics and software.
- ☐ The government-owned telecommunication sector launched digitalization of the Finnish infrastructure.

In the next chapter we show, how Nokia's defeat was turned into a victory. And how it is possible to launch a global high-technology product without any electronics. And finally we present two cases to demonstrate, that it is possible to become also a global leader on investment products.

Product business breakthrough: success stories

In news, and in textbooks about industry and economics, a common theme is the competition between companies and even between nations. The discussion is based on concepts like market share, customer segment, cost advantage and technological dominance. These terms refer to a strategy landscape, which is seen as a battlefield where roughly similar incumbent companies play the competition game with the same rules. However, when we discuss of breakthroughs where a new player is introduced or a new and virgin terrain is opened, a different viewpoint might be fruitful. We will now employ a product centered viewpoint.

The strategic play and balance are challenged, when a new class of products enters the markets, a new technology is being applied, and when a new and strong country enters the global markets. As was pointed out by Joseph Schumpeter, on of the leading economists of the 20th century, consumers are the ultimate decision makers. The product is the tangible change agent, which presents itself in public, and offers itself to be examined and tested by the consumers. We take some examples. The principle of generating light through electricity was discovered by Humphrey Davy, around 1800. However, it took about 50 years, before a practical carbon filament lamp was patented, and about 75 years, before Thomas Edison could introduce a credible product, and the incandescent carbon filament lamp was offered to customers - it caused a revolution in lighting technology. In this case, the innovation was most radical, actually Edison also offered electricity systems in order to sell lamps.

Most new technologies are not themselves products, but in order to be widely utilized, the technologies need to be applied in design of new products. In 1876, the combustion engine was not a product, and the innovation gained economical momentum only, when the engine was used to power a consumer product: the automobile. Transistor was not a consumer innovation, until it first was presented to consumers in the form of a portable radio. It also happened, that a Japanese company, Sony [24], bought a transistor manufacturing license from the original inventor, Bell. As a result, Japan entered to the global markets as a high technology exporting country. The world premiere took place in 1955, through products: well designed transistor radios, which the consumers liked. In the following decades, Japan, and then also other South-East Asian countries took a dominant position in the global consumer product markets.

In the previous chapter we discussed, how conditions for a contemporary industrial economy gradually developed and matured in Finland. We will now claim, that in 1980 - 2000 the Finnish industry entered the global world markets, and we claim that the breakthrough can be understood from a product-oriented viewpoint [25].

High technology for the masses: the GSM phone

During the 1990s, Nokia Corporation has experienced a rocket like acceleration from a domestic company in a small country, Finland, exporting bulk materials and industrial investment products, into a giant, multinational, high technology enterprise operating strongly on consumer markets. The Nokia brand has developed from obscurity into one of the worlds most valuable ones [12]. According to our theme we want to claim that this extraordinary success has something to do with good products.

Conditions for breakthrough

The company has its roots in the late 1800s near the village of Nokia, in the proximity of a large industrial centre, Tampere. From a modest start, the company soon evolved into a heavyweight multi-site national leader as a papermaker, and a manufacturer of electric cables and rubber products. In addition, the company was also one of the national pioneers in

---

[24] At that time, the company name was "Tokyo Tsushin Kogyo".

[25] Actually, one case product, Fiskars' scissors, was introduced already in 1967. In it's time, the product success was considered anomalous, and was attributed to "Finnish design". We now understand that this interpretation is incorrect. The global business breakthrough that followed product introduction should be attributed to excellent product engineering as a whole.

electronics. It started its involvement in electronics in the 1960s first by importing computers and establishing a computing centre, and later by initiating R&D activities. The electronics department designed machine control systems for the cable industry, and data logging devices, which developed into microprocessor controlled multi-channel energy analyzers. Nokia established the Finnish computer industry in large scale by developing and manufacturing electronic cash registers, which then led to a series of minicomputers for major national banks. Later, the company launched a series of PC type microcomputers, also originally for banks. These computers draw a lot attention because of their excellent ergonomic properties and clean and functional industrial design.

Hands-on experience in radio technology came from producing microwave radio links, portable military radios, consumer car phone systems (for the manually controlled national ARP network), and mobile hand portables for proprietary VHF radio systems. The company was a pioneer in the digitalization of telephone trunk networks by introducing the first commercial PCM channeling devices in the world in 1969, and later, after buying a share of a government-owned company, by delivering DX 200 digital telephone switching (PBX) systems, which challenged Ericsson's corresponding products. (Later, this technology was transferred to mobile phone base station networks).

A final technological ingredient before world-scale mobile operations was the introduction of cellular phone technology. This took place when the major telecommunication companies in Scandinavia standardized and opened the analogue cellular phone network NMT in 1981[26]. It became very popular, creating cellular phone markets in the Nordic countries, and cellular phone industries as well. Nokia became one of the major cellular phone manufacturers on Scandinavian markets. In technological terms, Nokia was well equipped when the global cellular phone markets were opening through the widespread adoption of the second generation mobile phone standard: digital GSM.

The world's first commercial GSM network was opened in Finland in 1991. On global markets, Nokia was still unknown and inexperienced. If we do not count rubber products, its experience on consumer mass markets was form the short-lived and unsuccessful attempt to enter television business via company takeovers. On digital cellular phone markets, Nokia was challenged by its serious Scandinavian rival Ericsson, and was facing

---

[26] It has to be pointed out, that the idea of the cellular phone and the first experiments appeared in the USA, starting from 1947. It is also true, that Motorola was the pioneer cellular phone company, which made many basic inventions and first successful designs. Motorola lost its leading international position for an unknown rival, coming form a distant corner of the world. There are different political, cultural and geographic explanations. But we believe, that without superior products Nokia's victory would have bin impossible.

the threat of powerful competitors, already strong on global as well as local markets, including Alcatel, Siemens, Philips and Motorola.

Features of the winning phone

Developing a digital GSM phone was a much more complicated issue than using analogue technology. Consumers were expecting hand portables - yet it was necessary to integrate into the phone several times more computing power than what could be found in typical office computer of the time. It took a few years until Nokia and its competitors introduced the first GSM hand portables. The Nokia 2110 mobile phone was introduced in 1994.

Many observers report being shocked at first sight of the Nokia 2110. It was so incredibly small. (By present standards, this 200 gram phone is not that small, but at the time, most GSM phones were closer to 500 grams). The phone had many advanced product features:

☐ Size:
   In addition to its small weight, it also had a slim and flat form. The Nokia 2110 was the first cellular phone to fit in a jacket pocket without trouble.

☐ Form:
   The industrial design of the phone was created by Nokia's top designer, Frank Nuovo, and was a true hit. The phone had a pleasing look. It had a large LCD screen, which could display four rows of text. The display was covered with a longitudinal, oval shaped plastic window. This oval form was the characteristic visual signature of the product. Overall appearance was smooth and round - and in sharp contrast with contemporary boxlike designs. The design was clean and functional, with a slight futuristic touch. An extra bonus was that the user could change the color and appearance of the phone by buying new front covers.

☐ Usability:
   The phone had a novel user interface, which is still in use in a modified form in some Nokia mobile phone models - and which has been imitated by competitors. It has two soft buttons, which work together with the large display, menu views, a two-position scroll button, a call button and a hang-up button (and two other buttons, which were later removed). The large display allowed a logical, menu-based user interface. It was not necessary to remember the functions of different buttons, but simply to scroll through the menus. The

phone also had a set of preinstalled ringing tones, and many of its features could be selected and tailored by the user.

It is impossible to prove the existence of a causal relationship from empirical evidence. Strictly speaking, we cannot claim that this model was the secret of Nokia's breakthrough on cellular phone markets. (Another important milestone was the invasion into US analogue phone markets, which was facilitated by a different model, the Nokia 101). However, the Nokia 2110 drew considerable attention, and sold very well. Instead of the estimated 400,000, the phone sold over 20 million units during three years. At the same time, Nokia's sales accelerated into a rocket like growth. Total phone sales doubled in 1994, and again in 1995. The final breakthrough of the corporation as the world's leading cellular phone company took place during 1998 and 1999. Sales once again doubled in those years, when a new record breaking sales hit, the Nokia 5110 was introduced.

A cutting edge "low technology" product

We continue by introducing quite a different type of product case. It is a most illustrative innovation example with several interesting features. This case prompts the question: what is a "high-tech" product? What is the product quality, the role of industrial design and the competition strategy in this case.

Our example is a product which is well established and traditional, and the markets are definitely mature and fully saturated. Still, the company was able to launch an innovative product with tremendous success. Considering the user's perspective, the new model introduces practically nothing new. The appearance and function of the product were not changed. Nothing at all was added to the user interface, to the way of using the product, or to the product's application area. The need for the product was unchanged. There was no social or economical change, which could explain the phenomenon, and no new market sectors or user types were invaded. Yet, this product became a worldwide success, which turned a small company in a distant country into a world class enterprise and a supreme market leader in the product sector. The company is Fiskars, and the product is ordinary scissors [15].

Fiskars and the tradition of shaping iron

The Fiskars Corporation has a solid and established background. It is among the oldest industrial companies in operation, in the whole world. It was established as an iron works company in 1649 near iron ore mines in southern Finland, in proximity of a village which also provided the name of the company. The iron works produced pig and bar iron for domestic markets and exports to neighboring countries, with a capacity of a few hundred metric tons per year in the late 17th century. It was evident almost from the beginning that the local ore was uneconomical to use. However, the location of the company was favorable, because of large forests for making charcoal, and a local rapid providing water power to drive blast furnaces and forging hammers. The works continued their operation using imported ore from Sweden, and focusing more on iron refinement. The works also made different pig iron and steel products such as nails, knives, hammers, ploughs, as well as pots and frying pans. In the 1830s, the company established a fine forgery shop and a machine workshop. They were then able to produce more demanding products such as tableware and scissors, as well as advanced machinery including water wheels and even steam engines.

In the 1960s, the company had established a good reputation and firm position on domestic markets, manufacturing hand tools and appliances for construction, agriculture, gardens and homes. It also provided a fair assortment of cutlery, knives and forks, and scissors. However, to describe the company's position on the global scale, it is enough to state that the most popular model of scissors had a manufacturing quantity of some 10,000 pairs per year. This was the situation in 1965, when the company decided to renovate its scissors production line.

Re-inventing scissors

Let us take a closer look at scissors. How could someone even think of reinventing this tool, which had found its applications and established its form from ancient times! Leonardo da Vinci had described manufacturing scissors, and practically the same process was still in use in the early 1960s. First, the blades were cast or forged and heat processed from an initial iron bar. The blade and handle were usually shaped as one unit. Then they were finished semi-manually using grinding machines. Finally, the blades were sharpened and connected together, initially with a rivet and later with a screw. Some top models were later chrome plated chemically to prevent rusting. Basically, the manufacturing process remained almost unchanged for several centuries.

Fiskars' primary intention was to renovate the manufacturing process: it had many phases, and a lot of human work was involved. Especially, grinding the scissors to their final shape was an expensive task. The company already had automatic grinding machines, which were invented around 1950 in Germany. Functionally, the machines imitated the movements of human workers. These machines were complicated, slow and difficult to maintain. At the time, numerically controlled machines were still to come, and the four degrees of movement of the grinding stone were controlled by several mechanical templates, which were tricky to adjust. The machine utilized a soft grinding stone, which left a coarse surface. So after processing by the machine the product had to be finished and polished manually.

The company's approach was to redesign the scissors to be more production-friendly. The solution was to separate the blade and handles from each other. Now it was possible to design the blade so that it could be processed with a machine with only two degrees of freedom. A simple and robust machine with a ceramic grinding stone could be used. It was possible to acquire a machine, which operated with high speed and excellent accuracy. The blades were produced with a tolerance of one hundred microns. No elaborate finishing or polishing process was needed, the blades were immediately ready for assembly. No other mass produced item except the ball bearing was so far produced with comparable precision.

The high accuracy of the blades was needed when producing the handles. The handles were made of plastic, and manufactured using high pressure injection molding. If the blade would not have had an exact shape, the plastic would have leaked out between the blade and the mould, and the process would have been impossible. When a prototype was made, the plastics company simply happened to have orange plastic material in their machine. Fiskars' designers liked the color, which became a characteristic feature of those scissors.

The new manufacturing process starts with cutting the blades of stainless steel plate with a mechanical stance, and finishing them by automatic grinding machines. Next, the handles are molded around the blade ends. Finally, the pairs of blades are connected together. Because of the self sharpening blades, a rivet could be used. It will never become lose by itself as a screw often does - and cutting threads in stainless steel is a costly procedure. In later models, also bolt and nut connection has been employed, made of high strength plastic

Product introduction, and how it was received

The new scissors were brought to markets in 1967, and were an instant success. During the first year, 100,000 pairs were sold: a tenfold increase compared with the earlier model. The company started to build new production lines, but the demand continuously exceeded their production capability. A new factory for scissors was opened in Finland in 1973 and in the USA in 1978. To date, the company has sold hundreds of millions of scissors, and the annual production rate exceeded 60 million pairs in 1999. The company is a clear market leader. Of course, sales of other products have also increased, and the company applies advanced manufacturing technologies and modern design in all their products.

There is little doubt that the explanation for the success of Fiskars is a superior product combined with an efficient manufacturing process. The company did have a well established industrial background and culture, but this is only an enabling factor. Why then is the product superior? It has won several industrial design awards, and the publicity seemed to concentrate on the specially shaped orange handles. As is evident from the development history, the scissors successfully represent the famous functional style of industrial design. Very little is added to the "pure functional form," assuming that such a form exists. Can the handles be the secret of success? There are thousands of imitations of Fiskars scissors. It became rapidly the most imitated product in the world. A common feature of the imitations is that they have orange plastic handles and usually perform poorly as scissors. For some reason, the imitators never tried to imitate the manufacturing process or high accuracy. Clearly, the distinguishing orange handles have helped to build the brand, but they do not explain the immediate acceptance by consumers. In addition, the shape itself was not new. Fiskars had used the same handle shape for the first time a hundred years earlier, but used bronze at the time.

Could it be that consumers are able to recognize a superior product? We would vote for this alternative! If a consumer is looking for good scissors, the overall quality and appearance somehow promise a good performance. The scissors look familiar, but at the same time very modern, almost alien. They are smooth and pleasant to the touch. The blades move with a constant, smooth motion, but offer light resistance through the entire working angle, and the sound of the movement is pleasing, not too sharp, not too coarse. The handles fit well in most human hands (left-handed and symmetric models are also available). If the consumer buys the scissors, he or she will find, that they indeed perform well, cut different materials and stay sharp. Therefore, a fair proposition is that in this case, the secret of success is indeed the excellent cutting performance with different materials, but at the same time, all the familiar elements of a good product are highly developed: function, form and manufacturing.

The success story repeated

To conclude the Fiskars case, we shortly discuss another product case, which presents a different approach (although Fiskars has achieved good manufacturability also in this case). The product is an axe. This is also an ancient tool, well established and mature. Users know very well, that a critical issue with the axe is the fastening of the blade to the handle. There are two alternate methods. In the Stone Age, axe makers made a hole at the end of the handle, and fixed the blade in the hole with leather strips and glue. An alternate method, which later became common, is to make a hole in the blade, to slide the end of the handle through the hole and fasten it somehow, for example, with a wedge. The advantage is easier fixing, but there are two disadvantages. The hole decreases the head weight and transfers the centre of gravity towards the user, which diminishes working performance. Another disadvantage is a safety hazard, because the blade easily becomes loose and may fly off with destructive force.

Another issue in axe making is the strength of the handle. It often happens that the axe user misses the target, which then hits the handle instead of the blade, and may damage or break it. For this reason, Fiskars selected a modern, very durable material for the handle: glass fiber reinforced polyamide tube. After materials selection was completed, strangely enough, the Stone Age fixing method was chosen. Considering the materials, the method is more natural, more functional and safer. Again, the result of the design process was an excellent product. Its impact on the company's success is more difficult to estimate, because it is shadowed by the scissors phenomenon. It also appears that the axe is less common than scissors, and more culture bound. Indeed, in different countries different traditional types of axe are used, and within one culture a variety of axe types are used for different purposes. The company manufactures several models of both scissors and axes. With scissors, the "classic" model described above is by far the most typical and is accepted similarly in many cultures, while with axes, there is more diversity, and no "classic" model exists. Scissors appeared to be the right product to start the modernization of products. Fiskars also redesigned its garden tool products according to similar principles, and again, consumer reaction was most favorable.

The mighty propeller

The other two cases are not really consumer products: they are business-to-business products, which are selected and acquired by engineers. However, in both cases, the product engineers have put a great effort to understand the requirements of the end product. Each of the products is crucial for the performance of the end product: a ship and an elevator. These products clearly exhibit functional superiority and technical excellence. But the products also satisfy the value function of the customer through a significant added value to the end product [20].

The tradition of shaping electric current

The Strömberg company, established in 1889, is the pioneer of electrical technology in Finland. The company has grown together with the evolving nation, and played an important role in the industrial structure. The company's special expertise is drive systems for large electric motors. The Alternative current (AC) motors are the reliable workhorses of the industry and society - but unfortunately, controlling the rotation speed and output power of an AC motor is only possible by changing the frequency of the power feed, which is not a simple task. Since 1970s, new power semiconductors and microprocessors appeared as the required core technology. The company has been working with two basic technologies for frequency variation: cycloconverters and pulse width modulated inverters.

The basic principles for frequency variation have been known for decades, but a static device (without moving parts) was a challenge. Building reliable, static AC motor drives for high power, up to one hundred megawatts, can be considered an exceptionally demanding design challenge. Especially, one has to develop and choose materials, components and designs for controlling the numerous secondary effects, associated with rapid switching of very high currents. In the case of Strömberg, the company's cumulated and long-term experience with motor drive power electronics was a considerable advantage. Motor drives were applied successfully in paper machines, steel milling works, and in electric trains, trams and metro cars. An important high power application is the electric power transmission of icebreaker ships, which are vital for maintaining the traffic to the Finnish sea ports during winter months.

AC motor drives can be considered one of the key technologies that Strömberg had developed to mature industrial level. When the company was fused with the multi-national ABB concern in 1988, the frequency inverter product team was given the global responsibility of the technology. Although industrial general-purpose frequency inverters were, and still are the backbone business, the Azipod ship propulsion concept soon became the high-tech flagship.

From ice breaking to luxury cruising ships

The concept of the azimuth propulsion for ships has been known for a long time. It is looks like a huge outboard motor rig, but the propulsion system is installed through the hull. The advantages of the arrangement are obvious. The thrust vector can be rotated 360 degrees, yielding excellent maneuverability. A separate rudder is not needed, but the drive is simply rotated. Also, there is no need for a reversing gear, as the drive can be rotated 180 degrees. Traditional implementations of the azimuth propulsion have been based on mechanical or hydraulic power transmission, which limits its use to small ships for special purposes.

Strömberg's experience, and advantageous properties of electric power transmission led to the Azipod® concept (azimuthing electric podded drive). It is an architectural innovation, which combines electric transmission with the azimuth propulsion principle. The electric AC motor is located on the same axis with the propeller, in a pod-like compartment. The pod is behind the propeller, which is pulling - nor pushing - the ship. This minimizes turbulence, and increases efficiency of the drive. Electric transmission allows very high output power, and its performance has been demonstrated in icebreakers. The motors of the Azipod are reliable and virtually service-free AC motors, driven individually by pulse width modulated inverters. Smaller Azipods utilize permanent magnet synchronous motors, which are cooled directly through pod walls by sea water. This is an extremely compact and reliable design.

The Azipod system means a revolution in ship design. With the new concept, the ship could be considered a power station. The primary engines, which generate the electric power, can be located anywhere in the ship. Usually one to three Azipod units are installed, depending on the ship type. The system has several benefits. The entire ship has built-in redundancy: it allows loss of a main engine (there are usually several) and loss of a propulsion unit (if there are many), with only slight penalty in speed. The propulsion system has a higher efficiency than with traditional ship propulsion systems; the advantage is 10 to 15%, and in some cases even 20%. Savings in fuel (and in operation cost) are significant. Primary engines can be operated with optimal load, yielding reduced emissions. Ship maneuverability is excellent, this is an important time saving and safety feature on crowded routes and in harbors.

Azipod's benefits can be optimized for different ship types. Electric propulsion is advantageous in icebreakers or ice breaking cargo and tanker ships. In icebreaking operation, a bow located propeller is efficient [27], thus a typical Azipod powered icebreakers might have thee propulsion units, two in the stern and one in the bow. A modern icebreaker can even move in oblique angle, to make a wider path through the ice. In offshore service ships or free floating offshore rigs maneuverability is the most important feature. An important application are luxury cruiser ships. The propulsion system generates less noise and vibration, and main engines can be located away from passenger compartments. Also good maneuvering capability saves time when visiting crowded harbors.

Azipod powered ships have demonstrated excellent reliability and efficiency. The innovation has created an unique and global business area, which is growing steadily [28].

Not an overnight development

It is important to notice, that a radical innovation, which the Azipod now doubt is, requires a long development time, and a lot of engineering work and practical experience. Her I can add a personal note. As a young engineer had the pleasure of working at Strömberg. I was not directly involved in ship propulsion, but in 1982 I was sitting in a coffee table with a few older engineers, and the discussion went to azimuth propulsion systems. At that time, a German company was developing an azimuth drive, based on hydraulic transmission. I can remember the conclusions of that discussion: we agreed that transmission losses of hydraulics were prohibitive for such a high power systems that Strömberg was interested on. We also concluded that a mechanical power transmission system would be plainly impossible. So the perspectives for electric transmission looked good. However, the concept obviously was in the idea generation phase. At least for me it was insecure, whether it was possible to build a small enough AC motor, to fit in a reasonably sized pod.

---

[27] A bow located propeller flushes the broken ice blocks backwards and away from the ship, and decreases friction between the ice and the ship. The low inertia of the directly driven propeller, and the fast reaction of the electric motor drive allow immediate stop of the propeller when it is hit by a large ice block, and starting a non-rotating propeller with a maximal moment. A special configuration has been developed for ice breaking tankers: it has no bow located propeller, but in ice breaking mode, the ship is moving backwards.

[28] Here we discover an interesting analogy. A morphological transformation of the Azipod drive is a wind power generator: an "upward pointing Azipod". Another Finnish company, WinWind, is manufacturing megawatt-scale wind power generators. The innovation has no relation with Azipod, except through the core technology: a permanent magnet AC generator, connected to the power grid by a pulse width modulated frequency inverter.

That was my only personal connection with the innovation. The next important step was when first patent applications wee issued and a propulsion system development project launched in 1987. The first drive system was ordered by the Finnish government for a service ship. A specific company, ABB Azipod was established in 1997 (now fused with ABB Marine). Currently, Azipod propulsion systems have a cumulated amount of more than one million operating hours.

The pancake that moves elevators

The last product innovation case has similar technology than the ship propulsion system: it contains frequency inverter and permanent magnet synchronous AC motor as central elements. And similarly, it is an architectural innovation, where technological building blocks are used to create unique technical performance and added value for product end users.

Thoroughly mature business and technology

The Kone company was established in 1910. It started with reparation and import of elevators, and then since 1918 it initiated elevator production. If we consider the product and the technology, the business area could be characterized rather conservative. The customer, the construction industry is not considered a high-tech industry, either. Elevator product novelties have been changes in the appearance of elevator cars and doors. The standard elevator drive is also technically speaking a rather straightforward device: a standard electric motor, connected to a cable reel through a worm gear, a break, and a control system implemented with relays. The elevator has a long service life, several decades. The oldest still working elevators are about one hundred years old.

What was the reason for Kone to renovate its elevator drive technology? One reason was the growth policy of the company. Starting in 1968, it had acquired a number of small elevator companies in different countries. However, as the result of the strategy, the company had to adopt and maintain a large amount of different elevator drives, all intended for the same purpose. However, the drive technologies had different designs and were mutually incompatible. To get around in this situation, it had to streamline the drive technology, and the starting point was taken to modernize the own technology. The process was started by implementing microprocessor control of elevators and elevator groups in the 1980s. This process was successful, and it also increased technological readiness of the company.

The new, flat elevator drive

A significant impulse for modernizing the entire elevator drive came from outside. The company learned, that its worst competitor, Otis, was experimenting with linear motors. Kone started also investigating this option. It soon discovered, that the linear motor concept had few advantages, but many tedious issues to be resolved. As a compromise, another concept was investigated: a flat motor, that could be installed inside the counter weight of the elevator. But it was soon found, that it is not necessary to locate the motor in the counterweight, it is much more straightforward to locate the motor in the wall of the elevator shaft. The great advantage is, that this arrangement requires no separate machine room. An elevator without a machine room is a significant added value for the actual customer: house builder or house owner.

But how to design and operate a flat motor? At the time the Strömberg company had already made pioneer work in the development of frequency inverters, and permanent magnet asynchronous motors had been "re-discovered" by industry, when powerful neodymium magnets had been presented commercially [29]. This combination soon led to the final design: a flat, axial magnetic flow permanent magnet synchronous motor, which is directly connected to the cable reel without a need for gears. The motor is powered by a pulse width modulated frequency inverter. It appeared, that in addition to space saving, the drive uses much less energy. It is also appeared to be versatile: the entire scale of different elevators could be operated with only two drive types, one for standard buildings, and one for high-speed elevators in skyscrapers.

Development of the new drive concept appeared most successful. The new concept was introduced in 1996, and by 2000 it had replaced all other drive technologies in the company's new elevator installations. Although Kone had already become a global company through acquisition of other companies, the new drive concept improved operational efficiency. Kone also took the technological leadership position, which is important for its image and brand value.

The business-to-business customers earn added value of the improved product. Cost savings are evident, because as no machine room is needed on the top of the building. Often authorities determine the maximum floor count of the building; in such a case, the elevator can

---

[29] Again, we discover synergy with the national industry. A government owned metallurgical company, Outokumpu, had investigated applications of neodymium, a by-product of raw metal production. Outokumpu established a daughter company for manufacturing of neodymium magnets - "neomagnets". The magnets wee adopted by ABB to manufacture AC motors and generators. The permanent magnet AC motor is applied in transportation systems and wind power generators, because of its reliability and high efficiency

serve even the top floor. It is also easier to assemble elevator shafts afterwards for old houses without an elevator. Energy saving is also significant, and fire hazard is reduced because no lubrication oil is needed. For consumers, ordinary citizens who use the elevator, the drive innovation is invisible. However, they might notice silent operation due lack of gears, and smooth driving due full electronic control.

Learning from examples

We have explored the success of the Finnish industry, and applied a product centered viewpoint. A company's performance and success is indeed a complicated issue. As we have described it depends on the economical and political environment, and also on the individuals and teams that work for the company. We have not described the product development process or the rationale behind management decisions. We have just explained the position and situation of the companies before the breakthrough, and explained what the success brought to the companies. We have also described the products, especially from the user's perspective.

We will summarize our four product innovation cases by discussing two important factors: the preconditions for product innovation and the contribution of individuals who make it happen. We begin with technological prerequisites. In the previous chapters, we have tried to describe the technological world. How it is composed of artifacts: different products and materials, and knowledge of using them - both everyday knowledge and professional knowledge. Finally, there are the applications. There are different everyday actions and needs of society members, in leisure and work, which can be augmented by knowledge and artifacts. There is also the possibility of providing commercial products and services to cater for the needs.

Conditions

It is often claimed, that incumbent companies have difficulties in renovating their products and business modes, and that they rarely launch radical innovations. In our four cases this seems not to be true. As we have described, each of the companies was technologically exceptionally well off. They possessed mature engineering and manufacturing cultures, formed through decades of hands-on activities with the most relevant branches of product technology. In the case of mobile phone technology, we also wanted to highlight, how exceptionally wide a spectrum of technologies must be mastered in the digital telecommunications sector.

Considering the companies' position on global markets, the situation was less promising. Nokia and Fiskars were practically unknown, although they had exported on a small scale. They did have a firm position on domestic and even Scandinavian markets, which in this case were economically insignificant compared to world markets. Regarding our business-to-business product examples, ABB and Kone anyway were already global companies, and known by their expert customers. Here we can assume, that product superiority indeed has been recognized through objective evidence..

We should also discuss the nature of their product innovations. Scissors definitely represented a mature market. The product was also mature: its form and application were established centuries ago. There were no grand new consumer trends visible. The consumers' need was to manually cut sheet-like materials such as paper, cardboard and textiles. Thus, the innovation was definitely a production innovation. The essence of the innovation was to improve the product a little, but most of all, a dramatic reduction of production cost and an equally dramatic increase in capacity. It is a good strategy - if consumers still want to buy your product, and if you are quick enough to utilize the new competition advantage before competitors.

The cellular phone for consumer markets is a radically new innovation. Who said that consumers even wanted such a product? Some companies did not believe it – at least not in time, and they suffered severe losses. Clearly, a radical innovation which is starting to gain momentum presupposes quick reaction, whenever one seems to be arising. On the other hand, the cellular phone is a very complicated and knowledge-intensive innovation. Technically speaking, when the concept was introduced in the late 1940s, the technology which made it practical for consumers - the microprocessor - was not yet available. When microprocessors became a common industrial technology in the late 1970s, there was still a latent period of ten years, during which companies and operators explored and prototyped cellular phone technology.

It is not sufficient to simply produce handsets. They require both a technical and service infrastructure. The latter includes base station networks and operator services. A global innovation also needs a global standard, and GSM fortunately became widely accepted. In Nokia's case, the company was on the front line, participating in the development and utilization of standards: initially the Scandinavian NMT standard, and then the pan-European and later global GSM standard.

There are two kinds of risks with such radical innovations, especially when they require a heavy infrastructure. First, the innovation may fail to develop into a significant business. A famous radical large-scale innovation, which failed completely was the Rapid Personal Transport System (RPTS) for urban areas. The innovation was a natural evolution of the urban underground train system, and it was supposed to resolve the traffic problems of large cities. However, although large amounts of money were invested, the RPTS system never even came out of the laboratory or the test track. Bruno Latour has analyzed the rise and decay of this innovation in his book "Aramis" [14].

Why did RPTS fail, and why did GSM succeed? Afterwards, it is easy to see, that although RPTS had both specification and technical problems - perhaps the most serious defect was lack of political support. A large-scale global innovation requires a social and technical infrastructure. With transportation systems, the infrastructure is to be built or at least coordinated by communities. As heavy investments are continuously being made on road systems and rail traffic systems, a completely new infrastructure would have required a very strong and centralized political initiative. Infrastructures may also evolve without centralized control and funding, through commercial product evolution. GSM is an example in which the international standard provides enough credibility and stability for commercial players to join in infrastructure development. It was also a new type of infrastructure; it did not have to compete with existing ones.

A different example is the personal computer. The concept of the microcomputer had already been established, and Apple was the leading manufacturer, producing well-designed and user-friendly computers. A strong firm, IBM, provided a de-facto industrial standard and made it open, allowing clone computers to be produced. This decision revolutionized computer markets, by creating an infrastructure of independent hardware and software manufacturers. It is ironic that IBM did not benefit from this innovation, but rather its minor subcontractor, Microsoft. We can distinguish several innovations in their start-up phase, which are facing the challenge of failing or being seriously delayed, if a large-scale infrastructure or a recognized infrastructure standard does not appear, e.g., the digital television (introduced already in 1986), the high definition TV, and the rapid automatic personal mass transportation system (experimented in France and in several other countries).

The next generation mobile phone system, for example the UMTS, is increasing its popularity. A few network standards exist, and commercial services are established. On the other hand, the dominant design for multimedia terminals, and user culture are still evolving, and there are some doubts about the future. New, internet based wireless services are appearing as a competing technology for proprietary mobile phone networks, offering radically cheaper data transmission fees, and as a side product, much cheaper voice and video calls.

A special challenge is that radical innovations are often associated with evolving and immature technologies. Competing companies often try to achieve technological advantage in product development by pushing the technology to its limits. Several companies, which developed GSM phones finally dropped the product, because the development process was too difficult or costly.

The human side of decisions

Managers and engineers make decisions, which sometimes are considered wise and sometimes careless. In the Fiskars case, the decision to renovate the scissor manufacturing method was important and fortunate. However, while the production of new scissors started, the top management had made a redundant decision to give up the production of scissors. The engineers had already given new assignments, and had left their posts. The workers of the scissors department insisted on continuing production on their own risk, and the rest of the story we already know.

With Nokia, the company history was even more turbulent. In the 1980s, the president of the company Kari Kairamo had created a strong growth strategy on the electronics sector. However, large scale arrangements, which included the takeover of most European television factories had disastrous economical consequences, and the entire corporation was in jeopardy. Fortunately, the telephone and telecommunications industries survived the crisis. The computer company Nokia Data was sold to ICL for a good price, but it took years to get rid of the television production. Another crisis hit the company in the late 1990s, when the explosive demand of GSM phones doubled the sales almost every year. The company succeeded to channel the demand with the help of partners and subcontractors, and avoided growing over-heavy.

Consumers make decisions, too. It is interesting, that we can explain the special role of our consumer product examples easily using the instrument viewpoint. Scissors are instruments for cutting. Cutting is a non-trivial task, but if the scissors are good, they are pleasant and easy to use, and efficient in cutting. That is, when a tedious cutting task proceeds well, the user is able to feel true joy and satisfaction in using such a fine instrument. The same is true for mobile phones. A pleasurable and efficient user interface creates a satisfying usage experience. In addition, the basic phone provides completely new and useful services: mobility, and a pocket-sized personal and electronic phone book. A new feature is the highly personal service. The cellular phone mediates communication especially with personal friends, and thus transfers emotionally loaded messages. In addition to being a useful instrument, it also becomes a personal companion. Nokia utilized this property early, by targeting their phones towards ordinary consumers instead of business users. This way they also managed to address a much larger customer segment.

A final aspect of our examples is that consumer acceptance is not only an enabling success factor, but can also become an accelerating factor. The "classic" Fiskars scissors, the Nokia 2110 mobile phone, the Azipod propulsion system and the compact elevator drive acted like the booster rockets of a spacecraft. The spacecraft must have a capable flight planning and control system, but the height and range of the final orbit are critically dependent on booster capability.

Wrapping up the product excellence strategy

A common claim is, that incumbent companies cannot initiate radical innovations. Regarding our product cases, this claim does not hold. But how to define a radical innovation? These product innovations were not really radical: they were based on existing technology, which was applied, adjusted and modified in a clever way. That kind of innovations are sometimes called architectural: they represent a new combination and new form of existing technology components. However, the product concept as a whole can be considered both new and radical in many ways.

Actually, modern technology is so complicated and information intensive, that truly radical innovations, those which combine new technology and a new application, are extremely rare. One landmark innovation of our time is the www. Even this innovation is based on ideas that originate from the 1960s, and are realized through large collection of existing technology - computers, software, protocols and communication networks. Another example. the mobile phone, requires many complicated technologies, on the phone side and on the network side. Such most complicated innovations are sometimes called systemic. They cannot be created overnight. Instead, they develop gradually, often even unnoticed, until they are mature enough for a breakthrough.

On the other hand, if the technology base exists and is narrow enough, even small companies can initiate significant and new product innovations. It is also possible, that a small company achieves growth and good market position on a narrow technology sector, and then becomes strong enough to strive for technological leadership. Typical examples are some software products and internet based services: games, web browsers, voice over internet products, and search engines [30].

We will now discuss some contributing factors to the transformation of the Finnish industry. We date this transformation roughly between 1980 and 2000, but it is also necessary to discuss the roots of change and industrial legacy. In the last section, we consider the new structure and its future in a global industrial setting.

The secret of industrial design

A common element in all our cases is the application of industrial form design. Even the elevator drive, which is never seen by normal elevator users, was finished by industrial designers, and the company used artistic photographs of the drive in its advertisement campaigns. Industrial design is present with Azipod, too. Although the shape of the underwater parts of the drive is determined by hydrodynamic requirements, there is a final touch: fine details, use and color of paint, and polished metallic parts. The evident message is, that the drive is efficient because it is in harmony with the laws of nature. In all cases, an aesthetic, pleasing form makes the products distinguishable, more acceptable, and helps to adjust the product in local cultures.

From users' point of view, the products indeed distinguished from the competing products. However, there was something more than industrial design alone. In a successful design, the form also mediates a message of performance. The real message communicates a promise from the manufacture: we have done a lot of work to design a perfect product, we want to show it, and we will keep the promise. But it is also evident, that in all our cases, the product indeed was excellent: it delivered a significant added value for its users. We could claim that the combination of pleasing form and sustained product performance creates a strong brand and reputation. It is an autocatalytic relationship: the combined effect is larger than the arithmetic sum of the components.

Why is it so, that consumers, and even business-to- business users, professional engineers, are attracted by industrial design? There might be some psychological answers. Benefits of product ownership and product use are not only related with the utility. A product's user has also a per-

---

[30] The availability of software technologies has even created a new type of innovation process: social innovations. User communities and enthusiasts are networking to create new value-adding applications and even products. A good example is the Linux operating system; presently the only real challenger for Microsoft Windows. The social innovation process is also sometimes called "open innovation". The terminology is not established, because "open innovation" has been used in purely industrial context, too.

sonal and emotional relationship with the product. It is an extension of personality, similar with clothing. Using an ugly or ill-performing product is not only a matter of reduced utility. It is irritating and even humiliating. On the other hand, if the product is excellent and admired, also the product's user shares this attention. This matter is well understood by the advertising people.

Continuation of the craftsman tradition and industrial art

There is another viewpoint to industrial design, too. Industrial design has been considered a modern, industrial age profession and practice - but it may be seen as continuation of an old handicraftsman and artisan tradition. It becomes evident by looking old craftsman created artifacts in museums. Especially acknowledged masters wanted to give the produced objects an aesthetic form and finish, as a proof of quality and as a personal signature. The masters often even signed their products. Clearly, industrial design and brand names are not a new invention, but they belong to the culture of artificial objects, generally and historically. A personal signature and fine finish are recognized and appreciated by consumers, as a guarantee of quality; why not to follow the tradition.

Was it a coincidence, that in the late 20th century, many Finnish machine manufacturers, as well as automation and electronics companies adopted professional industrial design as a default practice - and most successfully? Perhaps not. The Finnish design flourished in the 1950s- it became an international brand on industrial art. Especially the artists working at the Arabia ceramics factory in Helsinki enjoyed international reputation. Finnish factories produced everyday household objects: dishes and pottery, tableware, vases, and decorative art objects, which were manufactured in small series. The products of the 1950s are now desired objects for collectors. At the same time Alvar Aalto created a unique architectural language. It combined a pure and well planned functional form with personal style and visual signatures - typical signatures for Aalto were curved, s-shaped lines.

The functional industrial art style was a good match with the technical rationality of product engineers. As a result, industrial product design deviated from the decorative track. It integrated with the technically motivated form and functionality, yielding a total product character. A breakthrough in industrial design, applied in technical consumer products and industrial business-to business products, appeared on national scale in the 1960s. In Finland the visual language of this era was characterized by bold shapes and strong, deep colors. We can still recognize these features in many Finnish industrial products.

Creating a technical culture

We have pointed out, that to adopt, utilize and renovate technology, it is necessary, that we are surrounded by a very specific infrastructure: the technical culture - or technology culture.

In this book we have used culture in a wide social sense: a collectively shared way of behaving, and of understanding and interpreting numerous phenomena. Technical culture is a useful concept for explaining, how individuals and different groups cope with technology. Culture can be considered as a huge information repository. In our everyday communication, we can refer to culturally recognized objects, instead of explaining everything. Culture makes everyday life fluent and efficient. Culture, as a mental concept, is so natural for us that it is not easy to recognize. Driving a car, walking on the streets, using electricity, cooking etc. are actions which are mediated culturally. Except a set of adopted and shared conventions, culture is based on tangible resources: the presence of technically supported systems, availability of services, resources and everyday objects. What specific components of the technical culture were the most critical ones regarding the transformation of the Finnish society and economy? We like to name three: the education system, the industrial tradition, and availability of venture capital [31].

We have already mentioned the high standard of the Finnish education system. One result has been a common literacy, which is indicated by reading habits. Reading newspapers and books has been popular, and the Scandinavian free public library system is a unique phenomenon in global scale. We could assume, that literacy has supported formation of an uniform culture and shared objectives. Education has value on all sectors of the economy, and actually the first newspapers and journals were established to promote new agricultural techniques. Clearly, educated and literate citizens are most valuable as industrial employees. Although the higher education and the science system have not been especially advanced, they have provided a wide selection of disciplines. Even though

---

[31] Strange as it may sound, I like to consider the national venture capital a cultural resource. How could it be? Simply because during the early decades of industrialization it supported the shared objectives of the young, emerging nation. In the 19th century, considerable amount of investments came from abroad, but the industrial patrons settled in Finland and became citizens. One exception was, that the income from tar production and tar export created a shipping and ship building industry, which flourished form mid-1800s until the independence.

the higher education and science have not been of world class as a whole - of course there has been and there are individual, prominent Finnish scientists - it evidently has provided an access port for adoption of scientific ideas. In addition, it is generally assumed, that science is easier to transfer than technology.

Technological information is more tangible than science. It has been mediated by a centuries long chain of industrial tradition. Although the volume of the industry has been low, it has traditionally co-existed with craftsman workmanship. Finland is a sparsely populated country with long distances. It is necessary to be self-contained, be capable of local production, construction and reparation work. This attitude is applicable to technology in general: it is not sufficient to study it in textbooks, but you have to work it through, get your hands dirty.

The final element in building the technology culture integrates venture capital with a gap-filling technology policy. The early industrialization period in the 19th century was characterized by foreign venture capitalists, but in the era of independency this source drained. Small, independent Finland was not sufficiently attractive for investors. After World War II, the government had to take a more active role. The industrial structure was considered too dominated by wood products industry. It was necessary to balance the structure - the machine industry needed to be modernized, and certain strategic sectors were underdeveloped. Government-owned industrial companies were established for mining, metallurgical, chemical, energy and telecommunication sectors.

We have discussed some elements of the technical culture. But are these elements not really culture, or should they rather be considered an infrastructure? Why not, culture and infrastructure are quite closely related. But we have chosen to refer them as culture, to highlight the fact, that technology, whatever form it takes, does not work mechanically. It has to be in a living and active interaction with human beings, be they engineers, technicians or ordinary people.

Managing engineers

Is there a specific receipt for the Finnish engineering management, which could have attributed to the industrial transformation? There might be, but according to our understanding, little real research has been carried out on this topic. We will present some viewpoints, based on personal experience and on discussions with colleagues. Our suggestions may not be easy to implement, and they may not be fashionable - in a sense that they would be taught in management schools or discussed in leading business journals.

After World War II, the Finnish industrial transition was characterized by a shift from the production of bulk products, towards assembled, technology products. More engineers were needed to run the factories, and especially for product engineering. At the time, the management of companies usually had a technical background. Engineers were managing engineers. We regard this issue important and characteristic. A clear benefit was, that a similar background improved communication within companies, management spoke the same language as the product teams. This contributed to a cultural cohesion. A by-product was a low hierarchy, formally and socially. A possible drawback was, that the technical education of the time contained a minimal amount of management topics. Management processes at companies became under-developed, and many practices were improvised upon need.

A significant feature in the Finnish industrial culture was - and still is the lack of hierarchy. As an organizational principle, low hierarchy has been discussed in organization science. It is frequently referred in creativity literature as a necessary condition for innovativeness. It is also in agreement with the protestant culture and Scandinavian type of democracy. So it is not especially difficult to assure, that this feature really exists. However, it is necessary to discuss, how this feature is implemented. Subjectively we feel, that the implementation is more radical than one could assume - actually it might be an issue of ignorance, more than of implementation. We will explain it more closely. If one thinks of a democratic organization, one could assume a democracy principle in a negotiating, or a kind of conflict resolution system. But this is not the case, there seems to be no mechanism at all [32]. Management was direct, and based on factual issues, on the content of the work to be done. People are given responsibility on certain tasks, and usually there is a great reliance, that the work will be done. Or, the responsibility is not allocated at all. Only, the scope and conditions of the task are outlined, and the team then plans and discusses the details and work division, often without supervision of formal authority.

The case of low hierarchy already pointed out the lack of engineering management structure. But lack of structure is a more general feature, and actually we could call it deficiency. Our interpretation is, that the Finnish engineering culture has traditionally been based on individual

---

[32] Here is one personal memory. When I went to my first job as a young engineer, in the mid-1970s, I was first shown my desk. Then somebody brought me three or four thick folders, full of program listings, and I was told to "have a look". A few days later, one older engineer came to my desk and told me what I had to do ("find errors and convert the software to another application"). For this he spent some 15 minutes of his time. Of course, he was not my boss. It took me several weeks until I found out who my boss was. I went to talk to him and he said: "you seem to be getting on well". I have heard other similar stories.

designers, and that the management is person-to-person interactions, while processes are not properly recognized, documented, or controlled. Professional practices like project management and engineering reviews have been adopted rather late. Of course, project management and progress reviews were adopted properly on branches like the construction and shipbuilding industry, but application in product engineering was quite rare until last decades of the 20th century.

Although the work might have been loosely organized or managed, there was a strong motivation and commitment. We are inclined to think, that the high degree of motivation, which we have noticed over and over again, might be related with the cultural status of engineers. We have mentioned, that the 19th century education and cultural policy, motivated by political realities, left a legacy of a sharp cleft between the humanistic and the scientific-technical culture. In Finland, writers and artists have been true national heroes, not scientists or engineers. If one considered a technical or scientific career in the post-war Finland, it was definitely not to strive for fame, position or a good salary. Rather, the choice of career was based on deep psychological motives: a strong attraction or a personal mission.

Another source of motivation might be the tradition of low hierarchy. Participation and influence in product teams was largely based on capability and willingness to contribute. Designs were really brainchildren of the design engineers. And quite often, new products were based on initiatives of design engineers.

To summarize the character of the Finnish industrial culture, were have notified cultural cohesion, the lack of hierarchy, and the lack of engineering management structure. Personally I have noticed the lack of hierarchy in many industrial companies and organizations, no matter what is the size or business domain. It has definitely a cultural background, and seems to be natural for a small nation with shared values and objectives. But the issue of lacking engineering management structure is somehow different. It appears, that many large companies, including Nokia, which already had established international relations and had regular export of own products, had a more organized management structure. Regarding management structures, there is still a lot of variation. In the last decades of the 20th century, companies have also learned to improve their processes, and at the same time, professional, trained managers from business schools have been employed.

Maintaining the advance in global economy

The successful transformation of the Finnish industry is real at least in qualitative scale, and can be justified through explicit evidence. Despite the increasing international competition and escalating technological complexity, companies design and launched products, which are competitive on international markets. A distinct feature is, that the transformation was empowered by local resources. Although the world of science and industry is global, the transformation process was motivated by national needs, it was supported by the national culture, and it the process owners were domestic.

Some important questions arise. What are the characteristic features in this transformation in the 21st century, in those countries, which are now in a similar transition. How it takes place in many Asian countries or in Latin America, and in comparison, in Africa, where many countries seem to lack the necessary resources: education system, industrial tradition, and venture capital - and even the concept of "country" or "nation". In the Finnish case, the industrialization process was initiated by the appearance of the concept of nationality, which we see as a shared vision of culture and objectives.

On the other hand, national arousal, especially in populated areas, where many ethnic groups are living close to each other, has been also a seed for political conflicts and violence - an antigen for progress and development. Is it possible to invest on education and culture, without highlighting ethnic and national themes, but more general ideas, like progress (not really a popular theme right now) or a global citizenship and ecological responsibility? The international perspective is most complicated indeed. The industrialized world cannot deny developing countries the fruits of technological change. We wish, that this book contains material for this discussion: a description of the processes of technology creation, an the case study of the transformation.

After the transition, what is the future of the Finnish industry? In the era of global economy, is there such things as national industry or national companies? How can the Finnish companies - the most successful ones are no longer even owned by Finns - maintain their product excellence and technological leadership? In the current state of global industrial economy, companies are searching cost advantage, through externalization and outsourcing. Production is moving to countries where salaries are low. Engineering functions can be outsourced too - or even moved to whatever distant location offering a cost advantage.

From ad-hoc approach to defined processes and new horizons

The transformation has meant definite changes in the Finnish industrial landscape. The Nokia case is illustrative. After a phenomenal economical growth, which followed the launch of top products, the company was in a new situation. The company had to maintain and defend its new position. It was necessary to set up a high volume, well defined, structured and efficiently managed product development process, which would be capable of introducing continuously new product models to keep the customers interested. And a new challenge appeared: to match the product models with the expectations and special needs of globally consumers throughout the world. As we know from the continuing performance of Nokia, the new structure has been successful, at least until now. A remaining question is: is there still room for innovativeness? It seems, that the strategy of maintaining technology leadership and introducing innovative products still holds.

Similar changes towards more structured operation have taken place in other companies. They are now professionally managed, with well defined engineering and quality processes and product strategies. A new actor in the techno logy fields are numerous small software companies. Many have originated from earlier Nokia's sub-contractors, and they have set up at least rudimentary engineering management processes because of Nokia's requirements for subcontractors. Regarding the software industry, tradition plays little role. Due the narrow technology base, even small software companies can meet product standards and be competitive in global scale. The drawback is the hard global competition, and the global nature of software culture. The cultural advantage is not evident any more, and even the lack of hierarchy seems to be a universal feature of software companies.

Although it is difficult to evaluate, another important element in the industrial transformation is the mental landscape. The companies have learned to think and operate in a global scale. The success of leading companies has demonstrated, that geography of technological recognizes no national boundaries. Even small emerging technology companies are looking after global markets.

Is there a role for product excellence strategy in the new situation? Or is it so, that product cost is such a dominating factor, that the future world is full of products, which are on a barely acceptable performance level, but are selected because of their price? We would like to claim: yes, it has still a role. A well designed product is not necessarily more expensive - but it still makes a difference. However, achieving product superiority and technology leadership is far more difficult, because competing excellent companies have set new quality standards. And it is especially difficult with mature product types, where the general product form and pattern have been established. However, with new, emerging products, there is a great opportunity. When the product is still evolving as a concept, a superior design defines and locks the future form and functionality, the so called dominant design. The company, which is first to introduce the dominant design sets the standard, and is in a good position to take the product leadership. The others just have to follow.

The other issue is culture. We have explained the transformation of the Finnish industry partially with cultural factors. In the global product landscape, one could assume, that new products are developed in global context. This is clearly true with already existing products and with emerging new technologies. Technology is no longer created within individual companies, but in information networks, involving private owned companies, universities, research laboratories and standardization committees. And new product features are innovated increasingly in co-operation with customers, according the social innovation and open innovation paradigms.

But it is quite possible, that integrating, adjusting and applying technologies into new, truly innovative products may quite well take place locally, and be powered by some distinct culture and tradition. New dominant designs wait to be discovered and launched as products. For example, power saving lighting systems based on light emitting diodes (LEDs) exist as a technology, but so far, there seems to be no dominant design. The same is true with battery powered automobiles. Polymer lithium ion batteries - and a few other technologies - already allow lightweight electric cars, capable of a 1000 km ride before recharging - but we do not see them - yet.

Going virtual?

A few years ago, the research community discussed a lot of virtual enterprises. They are companies, which in the extreme form exist only on paper. They are legal entities, which do their business by orchestrating a network of subcontractors and partners. The subcontractors perform all elements of the product business: from product definition, to engineering, design, production and distributing. The core company has been left with the business idea, the basic strategy, contract structure - and charging the profit. Is this the future model for product enterprises? It seems to be, that recently many companies have evolved in this direction. Outsourcing and externalization of key processes leads to lean companies, which are capable of reacting quickly in economical and technology cycles. But there is a risk, that the company loses its touch with technology and customer needs. In product companies, technology has been a firm element in the industrial culture. Technology is adopted and maintained as a part of cultural tradition. Sufficient stability and hands-on experience need to be maintained somewhere. Our guess is, that some re-allocation of industrial roles will take place, but the direction of the technological change remains. Following the ideas of Joseph Schumpeter, we claim, that competition is still based on technological advance, and this advance is realized through manufacturing and distribution of products.

Is there then a future for technological development, or can we already see the end of history of technology? For us, continuing technological progress looks evident. New, powerful technologies emerge continuously, and they are both knowledge intensive and most sophisticated. And new challenges for technology emerge, too: we must fight global warming, create a new energy infrastructure, and improve the condition of environment. To cope with the situation, we need more science and education, and we need to create a harmonic technology culture, which cannot be separate from other forms of human activity.

References

[1] Alexander, C. Notes on the Synthesis of Form. Cambridge, MA: Harward University Press, 1974.

[2] Allen, T. Managing the Flow of Technology: Technology Transfer and the Dissemination of Technological Information within the R&D Organizations. The MIT Press, Cambridge, MA, 1985.

[3] Brooks, F. P. The Mythical Man-Month: Essays on Software Engineering. Addison-Wesley, Reading, Mass., 1982.

[4] Bush, V. As We May Think. The Atlantic Monthly; July, 1945, Volume 176, No. 1; pp.101-108. References

[5] Checkland, P.B. Systems Thinking, Systems Practice. John Wiley & Sons, Chicherster, 1981.

[6] Chesbrough, H. (2006). Open Innovation: A Paradigm for Understanding Industrial Innovation. In Chesbrough, H., Vanhaverbeke, W., & West, J. (Eds.) Open Innovation: Researching a New Paradigm. Oxford University Press: Oxford, UK.

[7] De Bono, E. The Use of Lateral Thinking. Penguin Books, Harmondsworth, U.K, 1986.

[8] Ferguson, E. S. Engineering and the Mind's Eye. The MIT Press, Cambridge, MA, 1993.

[9] Florman, S. C. The Existential Pleasures of Engineering. St. Martin's Press, New York, N.Y., 1976, 160 p.

[10] Gentner, D. & Stevens A. (editors) Mental models. Lawrence Erlbaum Associates, Hillsdale, NJ, 1983.

[11] Hitchins, D.K. Advanced systems thinking, engineering, and management. Artech House, 2003.

[12] Häikiö, M. NOKIA - The Inside Story. Edita, Helsinki, 2002.

[13] Lakoff G. & Johnson M. Metaphors We Live By. University of Chicago Press, Chicago, 1980.

[14] Latour, B. Aramis, or the Love of Technology. Harvard University Press, Cambridge, MA, 1996.

[15] Lund, R. 135+30 år saxtillverkning i Finland. Tekniikan vaiheita 1 / 1996 (in Swedish), pp. 19-25.

[16] Moran, T.P. & Carroll, J.M. (editors). Design Rationale: Concepts, Techniques and Use. Lawrence Erlbaum Associates, Mahwah, NJ, 1996.

[17] Negroponte, N. Being Digital. Knopf, New York, 1995.

[18] Nelson, T. H. Literary Machines. 93.1 edition. Eastgate Systems, Watertown MA, 1993.

[19] Nonaka, I. & Takeuchi, H. The Knowledge-Creating Company: How Japanese Companies Create the Dynamics of Innovation. Oxford University Press, New York, 1995.

[20] Nordman, K. (toim). Keihäänkärkiä. Kolmetoista kertomusta suomalaisesta huipputekniikasta. Svenska tekniska vetenskapsakademien i Finland, 2005. (in Finnish)

[21] Pahl, G. & Beitz, W. Engineering Design. The Design Council, New York, 1984.

[22] Polanyi, M. Knowing and Being: Essays. Routledge & Kegan Paul, London, 1969. 254

[23] Popper, K. R., and Eccles, J.C. The Self and Its Brain. Springer-Verlag, Berlin, 1977.

[24] Schrage, M. Serious Play: How the World's Best Companies Simulate to Innovate. Harward Business School Press, Boston, MA, 2000. References

[25] Schumpeter, J. A. The Theory of Economic Development. Harvard University Press, Cambridge, MA, 1961.

[26] Simon, H.A. Rationality in Human Affairs. Stanford University Press, Stanford, 1983.

[27] Simon, H.A. The Sciences of Artificial. The MIT Press, Cambridge, MA, 1981.

[28] Sterling, B. (editor) Mirrorshades: The Cyberpunk Anthology. Arbor House, 1986.

[29] Suh, Nam P. The Principles of Design. Oxford University Press, New York, NY, 1990.

[30] Ulrich, K. T., Eppinger, S. D. Product Design and Development. McGraw-Hill, New York. 1995.

[31] VDI 2221. Systematic Approach to the Design of Technical Systems and Products. VDI-Verlag, Düsseldorf, 1987.

[32] Vincenti, W. G. What Engineers Know and How They Know It. Analytical studies from aeronautical history. The Johns Hopkins University Press, Baltimore, 1993.

[33] Walsh, V., Roy, R., Bruce, M. and Potter, S. Winning by Design. Technology, Product Design and International Competitiveness. Blackwell, Oxford,1992.

[34] Weiser, M. The Computer for the 21st Century. Scientific American, vol 265 (1991), nro 3, pp. 94-104.

Index

www.ingramcontent.com/pod-product-compliance
Lightning Source LLC
Chambersburg PA
CBHW071307220526
45468CB00001B/290